Made In Heaven?

By

Rev D Kevin Jones

Or

How to build a better Marriage!

Made in Heaven?

By Rev'd D Kevin Jones BA.

Or

How to build a better marriage!

Published by "Heart of Oak,"

Published by

"Heart of Oak" 22 Chapel lane, Banks, Southport, Lancashire,
England, PR9 8EY.

heartofoak@safe-mail.net

Tel: 44 (0)1704 228394
ISBN> 0-9549462-0-0

First Edition published in United Kingdom 2006.

Printed and bound by: Lightning source UK LTD. 6 Precedent Drive Rooksley Milton Keynes, Bedfordshire, MK13 8PR.

The scriptures in this book are all from either the King James Bible; or the New International Version. Copyright (c) 1973, 1978, and 1984, by International Bible Society, unless otherwise stated.

Introduction

Again and again, I hear that couples who seem to be doing so well have split up. They may find another relationship, but often carry the pain of the failed marriage with them. Marriage seems to be under attack as never before. The UK has the highest divorce rate in Europe. Statistics from HMSO, tell us that back in 1930 only 4,000 couples divorced. By 1981, 27,000 couples in Britain were divorcing each year, 75% of these on the grounds of adultery or unreasonable behaviour. But by 1989, 164,000 couples were divorcing each year, and this has remained a constant figure in 2001, 157,000 couples divorced and in 2002, 160,000. 400 Children a day are affected by the break up of their parent's marriage. Each time I hear of another divorce my heart saddens at the loss, and each time I ask, could they have made it, **could they have built a better marriage?**

This small book is my response; it is not for those who are suffering a painful divorce, it is for those who want to make a go of it. It is certainly not about staying together at any cost. If your partner is abusive, violent or habitually adulterous, then the vow they made to love you is long since broken. It is for those who know they love each other but know they are not always getting it right. It is for those who will give time to their relationship and want to love with actions not just words. It is based upon life giving principles found in the best selling book of all time, the Bible.

Having been in the Christian ministry for 20+ years, I have prepared many couples for their wedding day. These principles come from those marriage preparation classes. Good marriages don't just happen; they come through applying principles of mutual love and respect. Marriage is the one place where people should find unconditional love and acceptance. These principles have been shared with both large & small groups and formed the basis of short radio series.

Marriage is one of the biggest decisions we make, so it is important to get it right. Whether you are married or preparing for marriage I trust you want to **build a better marriage**, one that stands the test of time. Marriage is to be celebrated not endured, and to get it right we must build on selflessness not self fulfilment. When we marry we must ask not what will I get, but what can I give? Love is always selfless. Marriage is one of God's greatest gifts and when we treat our partner as the precious gift that they are, then our marriage will be a place of security, joy, pleasure and friendship over a life time.

Marriages are not just made in heaven; they are very much built on this earth.

May you learn what it is to have a deeply rewarding marriage, united in body, soul and spirit! However good or bad things are at present, with wisdom and God's help your marriage can be rich and rewarding.

The first step is learning to listen properly. A husband once confided in his minister that things were difficult at home. The advice was: "Go home and learn to listen to your wife." After a month, things improved; the minister then said: "Now learn to hear what she is not saying!" We must learn to hear our partner's hidden needs, to listen to their feelings and emotions, as well as their words if we are to be the husband or wife God intends.

I acknowledge a great debt to the writers and speakers I have heard or read over the years, especially, Selwyn Hughes, Rob Parsons, Tim & Bev La Hay and the International Films course "The Adam and Eve factor."

Following the first three chapters there are questions which will enable couples to talk about their relationship. You can use these to review or discuss your marriage. If the principles outlined are thoughtfully applied they will deepen and enrich any relationship.

This book is dedicated to my wife, Anne-Marie and our five wonderful children, all dearly loved: Daniel, Bethany, Lydia-Anna, Joshua, and Rebekah.

Contents.

True Love!

1 Cor 13:4-8.

Love Never Fails?

What is True Love?

Three little words.

1: A Friendship. (Phileo)
The Priority of Staying Friends.

2: A Vow or Covenant. (Agape)
Love is based in the Will!
Love is never selfish.

Two Rules For marriage.
1, No Secrets. 2, No Blaming.

Love is not being too big to say sorry!

3: A Passion. (Eros)
A Sign of the covenant.
The Covenant of Noah.
The covenant of Moses.
The New Covenant.
The marriage Covenant.

True Love.
(1Cor 13:4-8.)

Let us be clear: when we look at true love, we do not mean the romantic "Hollywood" depiction, where Michael Douglas sails down a New York street with Kathleen Turner, (Romancing the Stone) and they live happily ever after, until the sequel.

The Bible tells us *"Love never fails"* (1 Cor 13:8). However, when more than 1/3 of marriages end in divorce, you might be forgiven for thinking the Bible is wrong. Is it true that Love never fails? Why do things so often go wrong? The truth is not that love has failed, but we have failed to love.

We haven't understood what love really is. We think it is just an emotion, so when our feelings lose a little of their passion, we decide we are no longer in love. I am currently the owner of a BMW motorcycle, when it comes to servicing the bike; I always turn to the maker's manual. If I don't, I have found through bitter experience that the bike doesn't run well.

God has given us clear guidelines in his word, the Bible, about how to build a lasting and fulfilling marriage. If we try to live outside his guidelines, we will find marriage never achieves its full potential. When we follow his guidelines for relationships, we find our society is strengthened, our children are protected and our own marriage is fulfilling. God invented Love as the very foundation of creation. When he had finished creating he looked and said *"that it was very good."* When things go wrong, we may go to the Bible for the principles which God intended a good marriage to be built upon.

Three little words.

The Bible uses three words to define what true love really is, they are: Friendship, Covenant & Physical or Sexual love.

Friendship. (Phileo)

A married couple must remain the best of friends; if they are always arguing sex alone won't keep them together. There is no joy in winning an argument and destroying your marriage. When friendship dies, it is no good arguing about who was responsible; both partners have lost their most valuable prize, trust. Husband and wife should give time to being best friends. Remember friendship needs renewing; it takes time to keep a deep friendship alive.

In wedding classes we talk about making each other a priority, and that means other things have to go. Hobbies, other friendships which over shadow the new relationship, excessive time spent at work: all must go. Everything must be reviewed and set aside, if it keeps you from spending quality time together. Couples must protect their relationship; nothing must get in the way & break up this most important friendship.

When the Bible speaks of a man *"leaving"* his father and mother and being *"united"* to his wife, (Gen 2:24) this includes letting go of all former relationships that in any way threaten the marriage, which includes parents and old girl/boy friends. When we ask in the marriage service: "who gives this woman to be married to this man", the father answers: "I do". He turns and places his daughter's hand in her husband's. He is enacting the priority of the new family over the old. He is symbolically transferring his fatherly covering, protection and care to the new family.

Marriage must be the closest of all relationships. Of Adam and Eve it is said, they were *"both naked -- and were not ashamed."* (Gen 2:25) This describes a deep relationship of vulnerability & trust as well as a physical nakedness. Couples should be able to share their most intimate thoughts and feelings without fear or embarrassment.

When a couple is close, each one feels valued and loved; they then draw strength and comfort from the safety of their relationship. When they are at odds, they feel unloved, unstable and undervalued. There is a danger that, as the marriage goes on and other demands encroach, couples will begin taking each other for granted. This must never happen! The Wife must be first in order of priority for the Husband and the Husband the first priority for the Wife. Anything that threatens the marriage must go. There must be a commitment to give time to each other and build an open trusting relationship, but love is not simply about friendship. When we marry we are making a vow. This kind of love is called covenant love.

Covenant Love. (Agape)

When we stand before God in Church we take a vow, traditionally: "For better for worse, for richer for poorer, in sickness and in health, till death us do part." This is a covenant made before God & man. It is a pledge to honour, cherish, and love each other till the day we die. When the Minister asks: "Will you take this Woman / Man to be your lawful wedded Wife / Husband? Will you love honour and keep them, and forsaking all others be faithful to them as long as you both shall live?" we reply: "I will!" We are not saying only on the days we feel like it. We are putting **our Will** into loving our partner, not just our feelings. This means Love can be directed by our will. On the days when we don't feel very friendly, or romantic, we have still pledged to love this person. We may be frustrated and angry but we have pledged to act in a loving manner whether we feel like it or not.

This is what it means to take a vow; we will not strike out or speak out in anger. We will respect, honour and be kind to the one we have vowed to love, not because we feel like it but because we have vowed it.

This is the kind of love which never fails. When you make a vow, it is a matter of honour to keep it. If that vow is broken, we proclaim clearly, "we can not keep our word; our honour and name mean nothing." We have no honour because we have broken the most sacred of vows.   When we sign the wedding register, we are signing our name to the vow we have taken.

The Bible describes this love in *1 Corinthians 13:4-8; "Love is patient, love is kind. It does not envy, it does not boast, it is not proud. It is not rude, it is not self-seeking, it is not easily angered, it keeps no record of wrongs. Love does not delight in evil but rejoices with the truth. It always protects, always trusts, always hopes, always perseveres. Love never fails."*

Can we place our own names in this description of love and say: "I am patient, I am kind, I do not brag and I am not arrogant, I do not act in an unbecoming manner; I do not seek my own way, nor do I get easily provoked, I will not remember my partner's wrongs, I will rejoice with what is right, I will speak the truth, I will not give up, I will believe in our future together, I will always hope and will never give in."

This is what true love is; this is covenant love, and this is the love which never fails. To make a vow is the commitment of a life time. On the wedding day we would never think of breaking our vow, but vows are made for the days when we do feel like getting out. Our partner should be able to turn to us and say, "You have given your word and signed your name, I expect you to keep your vow."

In the real world what are our homes like? We get up in the morning and ask, "How are you today?" "I'm fine", is the reply, when all the time they are thinking: "they should know how I feel after what they said to me last night." But we can't read minds, all we know is they seem upset. So how do we react when the one we love is upset? Do we go over and say: "how are you really?", "What's wrong?", "Have I upset you?", and "What can I do to help?" This would be the right reaction but NO! We think: "something is wrong with them, and they are blaming me," we harden our hearts & tell ourselves "it's not my fault!" Then we go off to work in a huff. We worry about it all day and brooding turns to anger. Instead of buying flowers on the way home we think: "if they say, sorry I will forgive them!" But we never think of humbling ourselves and saying: "if my words or my actions have hurt you, I am deeply sorry." The one who shows true love is the one who will humble themselves first. The one who thinks only of their own feelings is being self-centred. What has happened? Has love failed? NO! We have failed to love. We have not kept our vow! Remember we do not make vows for the day when everything is going well. They are for the days when we want to get out, but we have given our word and our partner should be able to trust us to work out any difficulties **together**. Vowing to love someone means vowing never to quit.

It has been said that lack of communication is the chief cause of marriage break-ups. This is only partly true. Steve Chalk said that "it is selfishness that causes marriage break-ups." When we get upset, we are too selfish to act with love. We would rather be right, than put things right. If we always want to win the argument we may ruin our marriage. If my anger, wounds my loved one, I was not acting in love.

Two rules will help every marriage.

1, No Secrets. A marriage should be a place where two people can share in open hearted intimacy. A place where they may say honesty how they feel, without fear of being rejected or belittled. We should be able to share our worries, our fears, our hopes and our temptations. If we are believers, we should certainly pray together and pray for each other. But sometimes we hide our feelings and this can turn to bitterness and resentment. We think: "If I tell them how I really feel they will not love me any more." So we wear a mask, saying: "I'm fine" on the outside but hurting within. Remember when we wear a mask we cannot get close to each other, because masks are lies in disguise. We must share from the heart the things which are important to us. No secrets.

2, No blame. The problem is we get all defensive. When our partner tells us how they feel, we think they are blaming us.

This means that when we share what we are feeling we must never blame our partner. An old illustration reminds us that if we are pointing one finger at someone else, we are pointing three at ourselves. It is no use saying: "I was angry, but it was your fault!" No, it wasn't! We chose to be angry, we could have acted lovingly, we could have controlled ourselves, but we chose not to. We must never dump our anger on our partner. We must never blame them for the way we act. Selwyn Hughes says there are two ways to respond to every situation. We may react quickly without thinking, a "knee jerk" reaction, or we can weigh up the consequences, measure our words and act accordingly. Do we act in love, or react in anger?

When we respond to our partner with anger, selfishness, pride or sarcasm, it is not a response of love; our partner will feel attacked and may become defensive. It may even be **_hatred_** which motivates us at that moment. Love is never selfish; the moment we are selfish, we are no longer acting in love. We have said: **"I will"** and we must learn to let our will control our emotions.

Ed Cole, an American preacher gives a profound definition of love when he says, "Love desires to benefit others at the expense of self, because love desires to give."

Some may have read the old "Love is" cartoons. Two cartoon figures with impossibly large heads are sitting on a park bench, and the caption reads: "Love is: never having to say you're sorry!" What rubbish. Love is: not being too proud to say you are sorry. This is what it really means to love someone and this is the vow that we take when we marry: to love even when it is tough, to humble ourselves and serve our partner. We have put our name to it and our honour depends on it. We must not win the argument and lose our partner.

Yet there is still one more kind of love in the Bible, Physical or sexual love.

Sexual love. (Eros)

Contrary to popular opinion God is not against sex. He created it. What He is against is promiscuous or uncommitted sex. The sexual union is meant to cement and celebrate the mutual commitment of marriage. Far from being prudish about sex, the Bible celebrates the physical union of a couple who are fully committed in marriage. To understand the place of sex in marriage, we must firstly understand the significance of the covenant we make.

One of the most holy things in the Holy Bible is a covenant, and each time a covenant is made a sign is given showing that those people are in covenant. Perhaps the most sacred form of covenant is a blood covenant.

The Covenant of Noah.

In Gen 9, Noah enters into a covenant with God. Following the flood, Noah offers a sacrifice and God promises never again to destroy the earth by flooding it. Then, *"Noah built an altar unto the LORD; and took of every clean beast, and of every clean fowl, and offered burnt offerings on the altar. And the LORD smelled a sweet savor; and the LORD said in his heart, I will not again curse the ground any more for man's sake; for the imagination of man's heart is evil from his youth; neither will I again smite -- every thing living, as I have done. While the earth remains, seedtime and harvest, and cold and heat, and summer and winter, and day and night shall not cease." Gen 8:20-22 KJV.*

Once the sacrifice (blood covenant) had been made, God then gave a sign that He would keep His word. God said, *"I set my bow in the cloud, and it shall be a token of a covenant between me and the earth. And it shall come to pass, when I bring a cloud over the earth, that the bow shall be seen in the cloud: I will remember my covenant, which is between me and you and every living creature; and the waters shall no more become a flood to destroy all flesh." Gen 9:13-15 KJV.* The rainbow became the sign that God and man were in covenant with each other, it was a blood covenant.

The Covenant of Moses.

Next, we come to Moses and the 10 commandments. (Exodus Ch 19-20) Here the promise was that God would take the children of Israel for his special people if they kept his commandments. Again we see that with the covenant there was a sign for those involved. The sign that they were to be his covenant people was circumcision, though it was actually introduced by Abraham. This makes the covenant of Moses a blood covenant and the covenant of Law is kept by the Jews to this day.

The New Covenant.

When we come to Jesus and the New Testament, we find that this time we are not in a covenant of law, but a covenant of forgiveness (Grace). God promises that for the sake of the sacrifice of the blood of Christ, he will forgive our sins and remember them no more. (Hebrews 10:17) The sign was given at the last supper. There Jesus took bread and wine, he broke the bread and said, *"Take, eat: this is my body, which is broken for you: this do in remembrance of me. After the same manner also he took the cup, when he had supped, saying, this cup is the new testament in my blood: this do, as oft as ye drink it, in remembrance of me. 1 Cor 11:24-25 KJV.*

Here we are speaking of Holy Symbols; the sign that Christians are in covenant with God is in taking the bread and the wine. At communion they proclaim that Christ has died for them, they look back to his act of sacrifice on the cross as the cost of their forgiveness, and renew their commitment to following him.

The marriage Covenant.

Now marriage is a covenant and it has a unique sign that these two people have pledged to be faithful. The ring they wear is not the sign of their covenant; that is simply a reminder. The sign that they are in covenant is that they may now sleep together under God's blessing. Sex has become the sign and symbol of their vow of love. This concept is reflected in British law since a marriage is not legally binding till it is consummated, and places making love on a far deeper level than a purely physical act. In making love the *"two become one,"* they are united emotionally, physically and spiritually before God. If the girl is a virgin on her wedding night then this covenant can also be said to be a blood covenant, as the act of love is sealed with blood.

The problem with sex outside marriage or sex before marriage is that it wants intimacy without commitment. We were not created for promiscuous sex. We were designed to share intimacy in the stable committed environment of a trusting relationship. Promiscuity wounds both ourselves and the one we love. When we cheapen sex we defile our spirit (1 Cor 6:15-16) and sin against the wedding vow of faithfulness. The Bible is clear, *"Marriage is honourable in all, and the bed undefiled: but whoremongers and adulterers God will judge." Heb 13:4 KJV.* Whether sex is before marriage (fornication), or outside marriage (adultery), it still breaks the vow of faithfulness and cheapens the commitment required for covenant love.

Chastity and faithfulness are not responsible for the alarming rise in STDs (Sexually transmitted diseases.) A recent government report said, "Risk avoidance and not the condom needs to be at the heart of the (government's) sexual health program's." Prof David Paton of Nottingham University, Dr Trevor Stammers and Dr Daniel Low-Beer of Cambridge University told a group of MPs at the House of Commons that neglecting abstinence has led to a "crisis in sexually transmitted diseases". Rates of Chlamydia had risen 139 per cent in 5 years, syphilis had soared 870 per cent and gonorrhoea cases had risen 67 per cent in women. Dr Low-Beer cited the Ugandan Aids and STD prevention scheme where teaching on abstinence and faithfulness in marriage had reduced casual sex by 65 per cent and HIV cases by 21 per cent. "Abstinence program's in the US had led to a drop of 7 per cent in casual sex and delayed sexual relations from age 15 to 17, Dr Stammers said". Source: Baptist Times. By keeping sexual relationships within marriage far from stopping joy, we cement family relationships and stop sexually transmitted disease. Sex is a beautiful and powerful gift, and like all powerful gifts it must be treated with maturity and respect. The 17 year old who drives a Maserati does not appreciate the power he commands, or the danger he is in, neither do people experimenting with fornication or adultery.

In fact, one famous preacher says: "Christians should have the best sex!" Why? Because they are committed to keeping alive a deep and lasting friendship, and they keep their vow to act lovingly even when they don't feel like it. With this kind of transparent commitment and growing trust, there should be few barriers to mutually enjoyable love making. At its best sex should be a celebration of the love two people share together. It should be a joyful act of thanksgiving, a time when we rejoice in the one we love and give thanks to God that we have been brought together. Sex is a sacred celebration of love, the sign that two people have been united to each other for life; it is too precious to be given away lightly and carelessly.

Sex therapists tell us that many sexual problems are not really sex problems at all, but relationship problems. Christians who work on their friendship (Phileo) and stay true to their vow of commitment (Agape), should be able to joyfully celebrate their physical love (Eros).

These are the three loves God wants for all of us, friendship, commitment and physical love.

Important Questions.

On friendship.

Is Your Partner the first priority in your life?
Are you maintaining your friendship?
When did you last go for a walk or meal together?
Remember close friends make the best lovers!

On Covenant.

Are you honouring your vow to love, even when you don't feel like it?
Are you patient and kind, or easily angered?
Are you able to listen to your partner when they need to say what is on their heart?
Do you listen or do you blame?
Is your love selfish or self-giving?
What are you going to do about it?

On Physical relations.

Did you know that God meant sex to be mutually satisfying and enjoyable?
Does one partner have a stronger sex drive than the other?
How do you cope with this?
When you make love are you seeking to please your partner?

Does the wife ever feel forced to have sex, or valued only for her body? How do you overcome this problem?

Will you resist sex before or outside marriage because of your covenant?

Is your loving a sign of your deep trust and commitment to each other?

A Prayer: - Father you have created us to love, and in your perfect will you have brought us together to love each other. May we know you blessing on our friendship, that over the years we may grow closer and deeper in love.

May we know your blessing in keeping our covenant, and when we are tempted, would you deliver us and keep us faithful and united in love.

May we know your blessing in our love making, that we would aim to please our partner an in doing so please you.

Thank you for all your gifts, of love thank you for my husband/wife; they are your most precious earthly gift to me. AMEN.

How to Build a Better marriage!
(Gen 1:26-3:17)

Some Common Mistakes.

1, Preparing for 50 years
2, The pressures of modern life.
3, We will always agree.
4, We will always feel romance and passion.

Does the Bible have guidelines?

The Principles of a good marriage.

1, Equality, Gen 1:27.
2, Different roles, Different priorities. Gen 3:16-19.
3, Fallen leadership. Gen 3:6.
(The problem with students, the silence of Adam.)

What can we do?

1, Learn to give each other priority time. (1 ½ hours weekly.)

2, Learn to communicate.

> The five levels of communication.
> Gen 1:25.
> Taking time together.

3, Learn to forgive.

Who makes the first move?

4, Renew our first love. Rev 2:5.

> Remember, repent & return.

How to build a better marriage.

Gen 2:24 "Therefore shall a man leave his father and his mother, and shall cleave unto his wife: and they shall be one flesh." KJV

Some Common Mistakes.

When couples are newly engaged and preparing for their wedding, their optimism may have certain false expectations.

The first is that the "Big Day" is the most important thing. It certainly is a big day and needs all the preparation we can manage, but if everything goes wrong, if the ring does not arrive on time, the groom gets food poisoning and the Bride faints, (all of these happened around our wedding) we can still build a good marriage. When we marry, we are planning for the next 50 years, not just the wedding night.

Another common mistake is that because of the pressures of modern life it is alright to spend long hours at work and little time together. This is a recipe for disaster. In ancient Israel, when a man married, he was given one whole year off work with no other responsibility than to establish his relationship with his wife. If we feel our marriage will be strong without investing substantial time in each other, we have made a crucial mistake. When we marry we vow to love our partner and love takes time.

A third mistake is thinking that we are so compatible that we will always agree. When we first date, romance tends to overlook the little problems. After a time, what seemed little can become annoying. Men and women do not look at things the same way, and we must never assume they do. John Gray has sought to explain the differences between the sexes in his popular book: "Men are from Mars and Women from Venus." Love does not change our differences and a couple need to learn to listen well, and understand that they will disagree.

Conflict can often arise through a simple misunderstanding. My wife and I will sometimes say to each other, "I know you think you understand what you thought I said, but what you heard was not what I meant."

Fourthly it is common to assume that a couple will always feel as passionate as they do on the wedding night; this may be a nice idea but it is not realistic. This will display itself in two ways. The husband will generally have a stronger libido than his wife, and if this is not discussed and understood, it will cause conflict and disappointment. The wife can feel used and the husband can feel rejected.

Lastly, it is not realistic to feel that neither husband nor wife will ever be tempted by anyone else. Temptation is always a possibility, but your partner needs to know that you take your vows of faithfulness very seriously, and are never going to give in to temptation. Adultery is never an accident; it is always a choice and always leads to destruction and pain. Adultery is a very serious sin, (Exodus 20:14, Hebrews 13:4). It is a sin against the vow you made to God; it is a sin against the trust of your partner, and a sin against your own honour and your own body. Excuses can never help an adulterer; confession and repentance can. (CF Proverbs 7:6-27 + 1Cor 6:9-18) Adultery is the one ground which Jesus gives for ending a marriage relationship. However if there is true repentance, there can still be room for reconciliation. (CF Hosea 1:1-6, 3:1-3)

Our vows are not made for the wedding day; no one would think of breaking their vows on their wedding day, they are made for the day when we are tempted. Love is not simply about feelings; it is a matter of the will. If we determine to keep our vows then we will act with kindness, consideration, patience, gentleness and faithfulness, even when we don't feel like it. (1Cor 13: 1-8) Our will can guide our feelings.

One of the things that will test newly weds is **finding their roles** in the new relationship. Does the Bible have Guide lines? Fortunately it does!

The principles of a good marriage.

Genesis brings us lessons from the Creator. From the beginning God built the principles of marriage into the created order. These principles are found in the first three chapters of the Bible, they have often been misunderstood and even abused, so we must tread carefully as we seek to apply them.

The first principle is that men and women were **created equal**. *Gen 1:27 "God created man in his own image, in the image of God created he him; **male and female** created he them." KJV*. In the original creation we see that both man and woman are made in the image of God. They have equal spiritual and mental capacity and they share dominion over the earth. (Gen 1:28) There is no inferiority between the sexes in God's original plan. Matthew Henry commented: "That a woman was made of a rib out of the side of Adam (is significant). Not made from his head to rule over him, or from his feet to be trampled upon by him, but out of his side to be equal with him, under his arm to be protected, and near his heart to be loved."

It is only in Genesis chapter three, after sin has corrupted society that specific roles are given to enable men and women to relate.

Different priorities.

I recently read some wall-plaques in a restaurant which illustrated the differing outlooks of the sexes. The woman said: "When I married Mr Right, I didn't realise his first name was Always!" The next said: "if at first you don't succeed, do it your wife's way!" The last one read: "Not only do I love you, but you're my best friend." Perhaps that is the one to remember. Men and women have different attitudes to life and different roles in the family. We will save a lot of friction if we work within our differences and seek to understand each other.

Following the fall, **man's outlook** became work orientated, and his family role was that of a loving leader. A **woman's outlook** is relational and her role was to be a supportive encourager, to both her husband and family; the Biblical word is "**a help meet**." This may seem disparaging to women who are still fighting for equality of the sexes. I believe that roles neither imply inferiority or subservience; they are simply ways to enable the family to function. Indeed, at times the roles will be reversed, the woman will take the loving leadership and the man will offer his support and encouragement, the key word is not leadership but love.

The Bible's perspective: following the fall, *God said: "To the woman, -- I will greatly multiply your pain in childbearing; --- and **your desire shall be to your husband, and he shall rule over you.** To Adam he said, because you hearkened to the voice of your wife, and have eaten of the tree, of which I commanded you, saying, You shall not eat it: cursed is the ground for your sake; **in sorrow shall you eat of it all the days of your life;** --- In the sweat of your face shall you eat bread, till you return to the ground;" Gen 3:16-19 (KJV modernised)*

Here, we are dealing with some of the basic differences between men and women. The woman's desire can easily be misunderstood. In sexual terms, it would seem that a man's desire for his wife is far stronger than her desire for him, but the Bible is not referring to sexual desire. It is referring to our basic psychological make up. A man defines himself in relation to his work; this is where he exercises dominion and finds significance. A woman sees worth not in her work but in her relationships. She knows she is valued when she is loved, *"her desire is for her husband"*. Her self worth and importance do not consist in her job but in the unconditional love of her husband. .

Next we find that the husband is given the role of leader, "headship" (Eph 5:23) *"he shall rule over his wife."* Even in Christian fellowships the idea of the husband's headship is sometimes rejected. In the larger world, it is considered old fashioned and exploitative, a throw back to a patriarchal society. Before we throw out the Biblical notion of headship, we need to see what kind of headship is envisaged, and this is explained in Ephesians.

Headship must be exercised on the basis of a love. *Eph 5:25 "Husbands, love your wives, even as Christ - loved the church, and gave himself for it." KJV.* A husband's love for his wife is meant to be sacrificial and selfless. It is only out of selflessness that he is meant to lead his family.

Fallen leadership!

The problem is that men find leadership difficult, and tend toward two extremes: dictatorship or indecision. One dominates, the other abdicates.

In the 1990s the chaplain at Cambridge University noticed a lack of young men offering for leadership within the Christian Unions. He identified three contributing factors. 1: That many young men came from families with an absent father, which meant they had no role model to follow. 2: They had been challenged by feminists and rightly felt that men had abused their position of leadership. The result was they were inhibited in offering leadership. 3: They had come to see women as competitors and were unsure how to respond. All this led them to weak leadership rather than being branded a chauvinist.

Adam's silence during Eve's temptation was culpable. "Where was Adam when Eve was tempted?" It is easy to assume Eve was tempted when she was alone and vulnerable. She did not receive the commandment to avoid the tree of the knowledge of good and evil; Adam did. *Gen 2:16 - 17 "And the LORD **God commanded the man**, saying, of every tree of the garden you may freely eat: But of the tree of the knowledge of good and evil, you shall not eat: for in the day that you eat of it you shall die. (KJV modernised)*

Adam received the command and was to take a lead in seeing it was obeyed. So where was Adam when Eve was tempted? *Gen 3:6 "when the woman saw that the tree was good for food, and that it was pleasant to the eyes, and a tree to be desired to make one wise, she took of the fruit, and ate it, and gave also (some) to her husband (who was)* **with her.** *(KJV modernised)*

Adam saw his wife tempted and did nothing to help her, his leadership was weak. The resulting curse was a futile struggle with nature. Work would be both his driving force and his curse. *Gen 3:17-18 "Because you listened to the voice of your wife, and have eaten of the tree, of which I commanded you, saying, You shall not eat of it: cursed is the ground for your sake; in sorrow shall you eat of it all the days of thy life; Thorns also and thistles shall it bring forth; and you shall eat the herb of the field; In the sweat of your face shall you eat bread, till you return to the ground; (KJV modernised)*

Man has had a love-hate relationship with his work ever since. The futility of unproductive and unrewarding hard work was his curse. Yet he still found satisfaction in subduing and ruling over the earth. The danger is that work becomes his only goal, and because work is difficult and time consuming, a man is tempted to put all his leadership capabilities into his work, and neglect the more important leadership of his family. When men first meet their opening question is invariably: "what do you do?" Man defines himself and draws meaning from his work. This is a result of the fall and is ultimately unsatisfying.

So we see the outlook and roles of men and women are different and were so from the very beginning.

What can we do to improve our marriages?

1: We must learn to give each other priority time.
A husband can only provide a loving leadership by making his wife and family his first priority. An over busy husband and a neglected wife is a recipe for disaster. Every couple should make it a goal to have quality time together each week where they can share their hopes, dreams and concerns. This time

should be away from the distractions of telephone and television. It should be "Our Time." As little as 1 ½ hours per week jealously guarded could make all the difference in saving a faltering marriage, or building a better marriage. We should actually put our appointment together into our diary. Why put it in the diary? Because if you don't, then something else will always take the time you could have spent together. Unless there is a commitment to spend quality time together it will not happen.

2: We must learn to communicate. Sociologists have defined five levels of communication.

- Social nicety.
- The exchange of facts.
- The exchange of ideas.
- The exchange of emotions.
- Total openness and honesty.

Of Adam and Eve before the fall the scripture says, *"They were both naked, the man and his wife, and were not ashamed." Gen 2:25 KJV.* This shows intimacy of body, heart and mind and is the goal of every marriage. A man and wife should be able to share their deepest thoughts and feelings without fear of mockery or rejection. This emotional nakedness we call vulnerability, it can only develop when there is a deep trust between two people. This is the place of total acceptance and love.

Communication is important in a marriage, but even when we try our different needs can lead to misunderstandings. A man arrives home from work and as he settles down to coffee and biscuits, his wife begins to talk about her day. It is likely that his mind is still at work and he is not yet ready to listen. The difficulty is he is in problem solving mode; his outlook on life and his work targets teach him to focus on problem solving. He listens for a while and then tells his wife what to do; if she takes certain steps she can solve the problem. To him this is obvious; he is task orientated and wants to approach things logically, the sooner he can get things sorted the better things will be, then he can enjoy the evening. However, the woman is not task orientated; she is relationship orientated, she was not asking how she could solve a problem, she simply wanted to be heard. The important thing to her was that her husband cared enough to listen to her day and value her. The result of this misunderstanding is hurt feelings and a sense that neither person understands the other. It will almost certainly have a knock on effect in the bedroom later.

3: We must learn to forgive. If a man wants to lead, he must lead in communicating to his wife how valued she is. Here actions speak louder than words. Communication is so important in a marriage. Self-centredness will ruin a marriage. When there is conflict it is useful to ask: who makes the first move in putting things right? If we are at odds, it is our pride which keeps us from going to the one we love, and apologising. We may even sit in different rooms thinking "if they say sorry I will forgive them", but never humbling ourselves to make the first move. This is not love, it is selfishness, and when we are selfish we are breaking our marriage vows. I would like to suggest that it doesn't matter who makes the first move, but if the husband is to take a moral and spiritual lead in his family, then it is his responsibility to set things right when they go wrong. If he is acting as a head of the household, then the needs of the others must come first. He must shoulder the responsibility and go to his wife to put things right. He must put his pride on one side and seek reconciliation. He must never go accusing her, but go willing to listen and to care; he must feel her pain in his heart. This is what it means to act in love. It does not matter who was right and who was wrong. What matters is that the marriage is strengthened. If his wife or child is hurting he must act; this is the cost of being a loving leader.

Love is not just about feelings, it is about commitment, a commitment to give time to the relationship and to never give up; less than this is not love. It may be laziness, fear, selfishness, pride anger or even hatred, but it is not love.

4: We must renew our first love. When couples first fall in love, their expressions of affection are instinctive; their love is vocal, voluntary and vulnerable. To spend time together and encourage each other is natural. It is only later when we take each other for granted that the fires of love grow dim.

Jesus tells us how to renew lost love. *Rev 2:4-5 "**You have left your first love. Remember** from where you have fallen, **repent**, and **do the first works**." (KJV. Modernised)*

When love goes cold there are three steps to renewed love.

Remember how things were when you first fell in love, remember what you have lost and determine to get it back. Once this is fixed in your mind, you must identify the ways in which you have fallen from this first love. When you see your failings, you must **repent**. Repentance had two sides, firstly it means turning away from the things which have caused the problem. Repentance is setting off in the other direction. It is more than words; it is a change of attitude and actions. Repentance is also a sincere apology for allowing things to get so bad and a pledge to change. Lastly **return** to those good practices which build up your marriage, **do the things you did at first,** "the first works." Give each other priority time, buy small surprises for each other, go out on a date together, touch without expecting sex, invest love in your partner and your love will soon blossom. Three "R's" Remember, Repent, and Return: this is the recipe for renewed love. Your marriage is worth fighting for, so give your best; make your relationship a priority.

For marriage to work both partners must consider the other person's needs as more important than their own. If we are in marriage for what we can get, it will never work; if we are seeking to give love and support to our partner both will find fulfilment.

If we ignore our partner, giving them little time, we will create pressures that marriage was never meant to know. Marriage is a partnership of equals, who work to bless each other, because they have vowed to love. Within marriage, each will find different roles and come with different attitudes, these should strengthen not break the marriage. The biblical role of the husband is to lead by sacrificial love; the Biblical role of the wife is to respond by respecting and supporting her husband. Where there is no respect and no sacrificial love, the marriage is not on a Biblical foundation.

Sin has affected the roles and attitudes of men and women in marriage, but there is no need to let our sins ruin our marriages. Through faith in Christ we may find forgiveness, and a capacity to love in ways that make our marriage prosper. Marriage is about commitment, sharing in intimacy, discovering our roles, supporting each other and saying sorry when we are wrong. It is the exploration of unity, of two coming together as one; the mystery of surrender and commitment to another person and about keeping our vow, even when it hurts.

Important Questions.

Does your marriage display equality?
Have you defined your roles?
Do you agree that man is work orientated and woman relationship orientated?
How are important decisions made in your home?
Does the husband take a loving lead in times of difficulty?
Does the wife find she makes all the decisions because the husband is ineffective? Do you spend at least 1 ½ hours a week quality time together?

On what level are you communicating 1-2-3-4-or 5?

Do we listen carefully before we speak?
Are we patient or dismissive when we see things differently?
Do we tell our partner how precious they are?
Who seeks reconciliation first when things go wrong?
Are you committed to making your marriage work?
Whose needs come first, yours or your loved ones?

A Prayer.

Lord God, teach us to be those who listen before we speak, help us to be patient with each other, teach us not to be so wrapped up in our work that we forget to love each other, may our marriage grow stronger and truer under your blessing. Thank your God for the one I love, teach me how to love them better, I ask it in Christ's name, who loved us and gave his life for us. AMEN.

God's secret purpose.

Eph 5:22-33.

A Mystery Revealed.

Why were we created? Rev 21:9. 1Cor 3:17.

God's Hidden Purpose Gen 1:1-3 +26-27, 2:18 +20, 22-25

Created to relate.

1: God is a relational being. Gen 1:1-3.

2: We are made in his image. Gen 1:26-27.

3: Marriage is a visual illustration of God's final purpose. Gen 2:18+20.

The remnants of The Fall. Gen 3:5.

1, God's image is destroyed.

2, Selfishness enters our personality. Gen 2:12-13.

3, Blame, Shame and guilt are born. Gen 2:7-8.

God's purpose revealed. Eph 5:22-33.

The coming of the groom. Jn 3:28-29, Mt 25:1-2.

Why Marriage is so important to God. Eph 5:25-31.

1: It is a picture of self giving love. V25.

2: The Bride is chosen by the Groom. V26. Ezekiel 16:4-8.

3: Love is a permanent covenant. V31.

4: God is passionate about His Bride. V31. (Songs 1:15, 2:2-4)

5: God Hates divorce. Mal2:14-16, Matt 19:4-9.

The Future consummation. Rev 19:7, 21:2-4, 22:4-5 + 17-20.

1. The Bride must prepare herself. Rev 19:7, 2Cor 11:2-3.

2. Prepared to reign. Rev 21:2-4, 22:4-5.

3. Reigning but submitted. Eph 5:22-23.

Still seeking the Bride. Gen 24. Rev 22:17+20.

God's secret purpose.

The Theology of Marriage.

"A man will leave his father and mother and be united to his wife, and the two will become one flesh." **This is a profound mystery-- but I am talking about Christ and the church. Eph 5:31-32. NIV.**

Behind the institution of marriage lies a profound mystery, a mystery which takes us to the heart of why we were created.

Why were we created?

In the Bible a mystery is not a puzzle to be worked out, like a supernatural "who done it?" Rather it is a spiritual secret, one which has been revealed by God in Jesus. It is understood by believers, but is hidden from those who do not believe.

It reveals the very purpose for which we were created. If we asked a teacher why they teach, they would probably say to educate children and give them the best possible chance in life. If we asked a doctor the purpose of their life, they may say to heal and comfort the sick. A preacher may respond that they are called to bring the eternal truths of God's word to their day and generation. But when we come to the question of why humanity was created, the purpose is greater.

The Westminster Shorter Catechism asks: **"what is the chief end of man?"**, and answers: **"Man's chief end is to glorify God, and to enjoy him forever."** Yet even this does not explain the depths of intimacy God intends for his people. Peter call us *"a chosen People, a royal priesthood,"* (1Pet 2:9) but it is only in the last book of the Bible that we see God's full purpose, when the scripture says, *"Come, I will show you the bride, the wife of the Lamb." Rev 21:9.*

The purpose God had in mind when he created humanity was

to create the bride of Christ.

This is the greatest honour we can receive. Believers are not simply going to heaven; they are going as the bride to a wedding. At a wedding, who are the people's eyes on? The bride! In Heaven it will be the same, angels and saints will welcome the bride. (Eph 3:9-10) But whose eyes are the bride upon? She looks only at the groom, because she was chosen to be his bride. He chose her, He courted her, He called her, and her radiance is the reflected glory of the one who desired her to be his wife.

We are of immense value to God the Father; we were created to be the bride of Christ, joined in a marriage union with God the Son for all eternity. This great mystery is hidden in the first chapters of Genesis, revealed in the Gospels and Epistles, and consummated in the Revelation.

This is why God stands so forcefully against those who threaten his Church, the bride. He says: *"If anyone destroys God's temple, God will destroy him; for God's temple is sacred, and you are that temple." 1 Cor 3:17.* It also shows why God is so insistent on the sanctity of marriage.

God's hidden purpose. Gen 1:1-3 + 26-27, 2:18 + 20, 22-25.

In Genesis, God reveals this mystery as part of the fabric of creation. Here, we find that man is unique among all creatures. He is the only one created *"in the image and likeness of God."* (Gen 1:26-27.) He is not simply a subordinate, but holds a position of authority. He is created to rule, with a position of trust and even friendship with God. God himself shared fellowship with man, in his days of innocence, as he walked in the garden in the cool of the day. (Gen 3:8-9)

Marriage is one of the dominant Bible themes. In fact, the Bible begins and ends with a marriage and Christ's first miracle is performed at a wedding. (Jn 2:11) The first thing God did after he completed creation was conduct a wedding! (Gen 2:22-25) God is beginning to illustrate his secret purpose.

Created to relate!

Scripture tells us mankind is made in the image of God. Which begs the question what is God like? When we look closely we see that God is a relational being. The first verses of the Bible give us clues to the nature of God. *Gen 1:1-3, "In the beginning **God created** the heavens and the earth. Now the earth was formless and empty, darkness was over the surface of the deep, **and the Spirit of God** was hovering over the waters. **And God said,** "Let there be light," and there was light."* Here God is depicted as a unique being with a three fold nature. In the light of Christian history, we call Him Father, Son & Holy Spirit. God (The Father) is the Architect in creation, The Holy Spirit is the life giving power in creation and the Word, Jesus, (Jn 1:1) is the executor of creation. Then God refers to himself in the plural as US. *Gen 1:26, "Then God said, "Let us make man in our image."* The evidence suggests that though there is but one God, he is revealed in three persons, and those persons are in a perfect, harmonious, self giving relationship. The essence of the existence of God is a totally committed selfless relationship of Father, Son and Holy Spirit. God within himself exists in a unity of perfect joy, harmony and peace which we call the Trinity.

The relationship works like this: the Father invests the fullness of His love and power in the Son; the Son wants only to do that which brings joy to the Father's heart; the Holy Spirit takes and applies the love of God revealed in Christ to humanity. Without the Spirit, we would know little of the nature of God. What we learn from the relationships within the Trinity is that we were made to exist in a selfless relationship.

Two things follow: **Firstly,** because we are made in the image of God, we are made to function in the unity of a self-giving relationship. We were created to relate. At the heart of the nature of man is the inbuilt need to exist in a meaningful and committed relationship. We were not created to be alone, we were created to love and be loved. Just as the Father, Son and Holy Spirit are in total agreement and a totally committed love, so we are created to be in a relationship of fully committed love. This does not mean that a single person has no joy till they are married. As Adam drew his significance and wellbeing from his relationship to God, so a single person may find their self worth and significance in a living relationship with God the Father. God's original intention was for us to be in a committed life long relationship, but this does not mean all people will marry. (CF 1Cor 7:7-9) God's original plan is stated clearly in Genesis, *"the LORD God said, It is not good that the man should be alone; Therefore shall a man leave his father and his mother, and shall cleave unto his wife: and they shall be one flesh." Gen 2:18 + 24 KJV*

Secondly, we need to remember that marriage is a visual illustration of God's final intention, of creating from humanity, the bride of Christ. This is illustrated when God forms a suitable partner for Adam. *Gen 2:18 "I will make a helper suitable (Comparable to) him." Gen 2:20 But for Adam no suitable helper was found." NIV*

God desires to share the perfection of His self-giving love with someone capable of appreciating it. Just as there was no comparable partner for Adam, so there was no one comparable to God. Before time came into being, God existed in perfect joy, unity and love. He wanted to draw someone into that relationship so that they could share in the fullness of all He is. And because there was no one he could lavish His love upon, He created someone in *"his own image and likeness."* Mankind was created to appreciate and enjoy the love of God forever, but they were never ready to take up this great position, because they were still in their infancy. It was only as they "came of age" that they could have appreciated the fullness of God's purpose. The history of faith can be seen as our response to the call of the groom: *Song 2:13 "Arise, my love, my fair one, and come away." KJV.*

He calls us and courts us, through His Word and by His Spirit; we are invited not to the wedding but to be His bride.

The remnants of the fall.

The fall perverted God's plan but could only postpone the marriage. The original temptation promised equality with God. Gen 3:5. Says, *"God knows that when you eat of it your eyes will be opened, and you will **be like God**, knowing good and evil."*

This was a lie; man was already like God, made in God's image. The fall marred that image. We became unlike God, being self-centred rather than selfless. We became prey to the experience of evil, which God never intended. To KNOW good and evil means to experience good and evil. God intended that mankind should only experience good. When sin entered our personality and dominion, we became open to good and evil forces. Before we could be reunited with a wholly good creator, sin had to be dealt with.

Man's relationship with God was broken. Instead of confessing his fault, he tries to shift the blame. Selfishness and shame enters his relationships (Gen 2:7-8 +12-13). Between the first man and his wife there had been total open-hearted commitment, they had shared deeply in body, soul and spirit. They had been able to share their deepest feelings and desires openly and had always been fully concerned with each other's needs. Because mankind was created to be self-giving, it had been their delight to fulfil their partner in every way. The first couple would never have asked: "what can I get out of this?", but: "what can I give to make my loved one happy?"

Now once sin created selfishness, then as certain as the dawn, accusation, recrimination, guilt and shame followed. Instead of man being selfless and loving, we became selfish and taking. Unless a marriage returns to the principle of self-giving love, it will never be all God intended. Selfishness is now so much a part of our personality that we will need God's help if we are to begin putting our partner first. Only by receiving God's life giving Spirit and obeying God's living word, can we become more aware of our partner's needs than our own. When we find we are selfish, we must never make excuses but apologize and seek to put things right.

Too many marriages exist with one partner being deeply unsatisfied and the other unconcerned or unaware of the problem. We must learn to speak openly without blaming each other, and seek to lovingly meet each other's emotional, spiritual and physical needs. As God is totally devoted to the wellbeing of his people, so we must be devoted to the wellbeing of our partners.

Even now God has not abandoned His people. God's desire in creating mankind was to find someone he could centre his love upon, who would freely return that love. Our name for someone like that is a bride. Christian marriages at their best should be a depiction of the selfless love which God has for us. Through his power we should learn to love not only with our strength but with the love of the Lord.

We were created to glorify God and to enjoy him forever. The commitment of human marriage is a picture of how much God loves his people. A good marriage based on selfless love gives us a glimpse of the commitment God has to us. When we see forgiveness in the eyes of our partner, we have a glimpse into the heart of God. When they accept us even with our faults we receive grace (unmerited favour) and grace is at the very heart of God. All forgiving love resides at the heart of the nature of God. Marriage is a visual aid to the final union of Christ and His Church.

God's Purpose Revealed! Eph 5:22-33.

In the New Testament three witnesses combine to reveal that the groom has arrived: John the Baptist, Jesus and Paul; all speak of the bridegroom.

In Christ, the Bridegroom has come to seek His bride.

John the Baptist said, *John 3:28-29, "'I am not the Christ but am sent ahead of him.' The bride belongs to the bridegroom. The friend who attends the bridegroom waits and listens for him, and is full of joy when he hears the bridegroom's voice. That joy is mine, and it is now complete." NIV*

Jesus compares himself to the Bridegroom, in the parable of the ten virgins. *"At that time the kingdom of heaven will be like ten virgins who took their lamps and went out to meet the bridegroom. Five of them were foolish and five were wise." Matt 25:1-2.*

Then, in Ephesians, **Paul** reveals the mystery behind marriage. He says: *"Husbands, love your wives, **just as Christ loved the church** and gave himself up for her to make her holy, cleansing her by the washing with water through the word, --- This is a profound mystery-- but I am talking about Christ and the church." Eph 5:25-26+32 NIV.*

The selfless commitment that Christ showed to his Church is the measure of the commitment we should bring to our marriages. In Ephesians 5 the commitment of husband and wife pre-figure the commitment of Christ to His Church. Until we see that God's purpose is the union of Christ and his Church, we cannot fully appreciate the covenant of marriage. Christ is totally committed to His bride. This means we should be totally committed to our marriage partner.

Now we begin to understand why marriage is so important to God.

1, It is a picture of self-giving love. As Christ *gave*

himself up, (v25) so the husband is to give up his rights and selfish desires so that his wife may find fulfilment. The idea here is of giving up one's own rights to gain a better relationship. It is one many marriages would benefit from. The example is Christ's sacrificial love upon the cross, though he did not wish to go to Calvary; he prayed: *"Not my will, but yours be done." Luke 22:42. NIV.* It is with the same spirit of self sacrifice that a husband is called to serve his wife.

2, The bride was chosen, *"that He might Sanctify and cleanse her." (v26)* Christ did not choose his bride because of her beauty or intelligence. It was not some greatness in us that attracted the groom; it was the decision of his heart to love the unlovely. We are chosen because of his love not because of our loveliness. How unlike us, we choose a bride or groom because of their appearance, their femininity or masculinity, or it may be some other competence that attracts us, their wit or wealth, then when that is gone, we are no longer attracted.

This idea of God choosing the unlovely is illustrated in Israel's history. *Ezek 16:4-8*

"On the day you were born your cord was not cut, nor were you washed with water to make you clean, nor were you rubbed with salt or wrapped in cloths. No-one looked on you with pity or had compassion enough to do any of these things for you. Rather, you were thrown out into the open field, for on the day you were born you were despised. Then I passed by and saw you kicking about in your blood, and as you lay there in your blood I said to you, "Live!" I made you grow like a plant of the field. You grew up and developed and became the most beautiful of jewels. Your breasts were formed and your hair grew, you who were naked and bare. "Later I passed by, and when I looked at you and saw that you were old enough for love, I spread the corner of my garment over you and covered your nakedness. I gave you my solemn oath and entered into a covenant with you, declares the Sovereign LORD, and you became mine. NIV.

This is part of the mystery of God's love, the groom chooses the bride. He chooses and we respond. The scripture says: *"We love Him because He first loved us." 1John 4:19 KJV.* It is His love that draws the best out of us. We were chosen in order to **sanctify and cleanse** us. (v26) So it is in marriage, when we love in order to beautify our partner, rather than because they are beautiful, then their love grows in response and their hidden beauty comes forward. Seek to genuinely compliment your partner when they show their love and you will soon see the best coming out of them. Adversely watch the response when you complain and criticize. Encouragement prompts love, criticism brings insecurity and anger.

3, Love is a public covenant. *"The man will leave his father and mother and be joined to his wife".* (v31) The commitment of marriage symbolizes God's commitment to us. We enact the permanence of this covenant when we ask "who gives this woman to be married to this man?" And the father gives his daughter away. The prophet asks: *"Can a mother forget the baby at her breast and have no compassion on the child she has borne? Though she may forget, I will not forget you! See, I have engraved you on the palms of my hands;" Isa 49:15-16 NIV.*

God is absolutely committed to His bride and expects the same commitment of us. Jesus said: *"A man shall leave his father and mother, and cleave to his wife; and the two shall be one flesh: so then they are no more two, but one flesh. **What therefore God hath joined together, let not man put asunder".** Mark 10:7-9, KJV.*

God loves us unconditionally. The theologians call this love, un-caused and un-affected. It did not spring from anything in us, and it can not be affected by any action we take. God will not love us less if we sin, he will not love us more if we are faithful. His love is constant; however our experience of his love may differ. Our response to his love will reveal whether we are truly part of the bride of Christ. If we do not love him in return we have no part in his kingdom.

4, God is passionate about the love of His beloved.
"And the two shall become one." (Eph 5v31) We find
the ultimate expression of God's passion in the Song of
Solomon. Here we see that the lover represents Christ and the
beloved His bride the Church. The lover calls: *"How beautiful
you are, my darling! Oh, how beautiful! Your eyes are doves."
Song 1:15.* The Beloved responds: *"Like a lily among thorns is
my darling among the maidens. Like an apple tree among
the trees of the forest is my lover among the young men. I
delight to sit in his shade, and his fruit is sweet to my taste. He
has taken me to the banquet hall, and his banner over me is
love. Song 2:2-4.*

He describes her beauty in great detail. *Song 4:1-5, "How
beautiful you are, my darling! Oh, how beautiful! Your eyes
behind your veil are doves. Your hair is like a flock of goats
descending from Mount Gilead. Your teeth are like a flock of
sheep just shorn, coming up from the washing. Each has its
twin; not one of them is alone. Your lips are like a scarlet
ribbon; your mouth is lovely. Your temples behind your veil
are like the halves of a pomegranate. Your neck is like the
tower of David, built with elegance; on it hang a thousand
shields, all of them shields of warriors. Your two breasts are
like two fawns, like twin fawns of a gazelle that browse
among the lilies.*

God is passionate about His people. He is committed to
bringing them faultless before his throne with great joy. (Jude
24) The passionate embrace of young lovers tells us something
of what it will be like to be welcomed into the kingdom of
heaven. God also expects us to be passionate about each other
and the commitment of marriage is the place where that
passion is to be shared.

5, God hates divorce. It mars the image God intended of
his unshakable commitment to his bride. In Malachi, God
speaks plainly about divorce. *"The LORD is acting as the
witness between you and the wife of your youth, because you*

have broken faith with her, though she is your partner, the wife of your marriage covenant. Has not [the LORD] made them one? In flesh and spirit, --- So guard yourself in your spirit, and do not break faith with the wife of your youth. **"I hate divorce," says the LORD God of Israel."** *Mal 2:14-16*

Because divorce is so common today we tend to rationalize it as an acceptable option. Irreconcilable difficulties or estrangement and adultery, are the most common reasons for divorce, followed by adultery. But surely it would be better to love as Christ intends and with His help, keep our vows. In God's eyes the covenant vowed on our wedding day is holy and binding, in His eyes we marry "till death do us part." Since marriage is essentially a physical act, it can only be broken by a physical act: adultery. This does not mean that God will reject those who are divorced, but it does mean that divorce was never part of God's best will and plan for our lives. Adulterers in breaking their vows sign their own divorce decree. Only through confession & repentance can they find healing.

In Christ's days on earth, divorce was almost as common, as today. Jesus said it came through hardness of heart, and acting in our own self-interest. Selfishness is often the root cause of a marriage breakdown. When someone thinks they are right, pride stops them from humbling themselves and going in love to the partner they have pledged to love. They become hard-hearted. *Matt 19:4f,* The Pharisees asked Jesus *"Why - did Moses command that a man give his wife a certificate of divorce and send her away?" Jesus replied,* **"Moses permitted** *you to divorce your wives* **because your hearts were hard.** *But it was not this way from the beginning. I tell you that anyone who divorces his wife, except for marital unfaithfulness, and marries another woman commits adultery."* Adultery destroys the exclusive basis of the marriage covenant. Sex outside marriage is the sure route to destroying both your marriage and your spiritual life. (CF Proverbs Ch 5) The adulterer has already divorced him or herself from their vow, here the innocent party may leave without any fear of sin.

Incompatibility is no real excuse for divorce. We must align ourselves with God's word; instead of accepting our differences and hardening our hearts. We should LOVE with our will! This way we are fulfilling our vows. **We cannot say that our love has failed when we have actually failed to love.** Love covers a multitude of sins and love never fails. (1 Cor 13:8) If we will commit ourselves to loving our partner in spite of our feelings then soon enough our feelings will revive.

Divorce should not be a topic of conversation for Christians; it sows seeds of doubt and undermines trust. Our partner needs to know that when things are tough we are committed to working it out together. We should not deceive ourselves that divorce will be amicable, when lawyers and finances are involved, it causes pain. Within all of us is the capacity to do each other harm, if we release it, we will harm ourselves and those we vowed to love. Even the best of people are deeply wounded by divorce; it is not an easy option. Strong men and strong women can be hardened through divorce; when we loose the one we love we lose something of our self worth too. Better to communicate or concerns than run in haste. We have vowed to love, not to give up. The Biblical exceptions are few: adultery, violence, (which is a sin against love) and possibly abandonment. (1 Cor 7:15)

Healing is possible. So far we have been encouraging couples seeking to avoid divorce. Yet, so many find they have a failed marriage, when they never thought it could happen to them. Is there any hope for one who has been divorced? The answer is yes, healing is possible.

This book concentrates on the ideal, but we live in a far from ideal world. Though divorce was not God's best plan for you, it does not mean you must miss out on His blessing or future happiness. God does not condemn us for our past. The great King David, (2Sam Ch 11+12) committed adultery taking another mans wife; But when he was confronted with his sin he confesses all in deep sorrow, and found that God was still willing to forgive and restore him. In fact, it was one of David's and Bathsheba's Children that became the greatest ever king of Israel, King Solomon. God asks one thing; have you sought forgiveness and cleansing from Jesus for your part in the divorce? At this stage, we can not ask what the other person did, to provoke us, what matters is making our heart clean in God's sight. If you have not sought God's gracious forgiveness, stop reading and seek Him today, don't carry needless guilt. The "prayer for those who want to follow Christ" may be of help to some, you will find it at the end of this section.

Once you have sought forgiveness from God, then your past is behind you and you have a new future ahead. The question is not where you have come from but where you stand today and what you will do in the future. If you are a believer, God has not rejected you, you are has his child. His aim is to grant to each of us His overwhelming love and forgiveness. He seeks only to restore, to heal and to cleanse us from our past, whether we were the innocent or the guilty party. If you are re-married God is not asking you to return to your first partner (CF Deut 24:1-4). He asks you to show true devotion and commitment to your present partner. He expects you to love with a selfless covenant love and not to make the same mistakes again.

If we live together as man & wife without being married, we should ask, why are we unwilling to make a covenant commitment? Marriage is the mutual sealing with binding vows of the commitment we feel in our hearts. It is a Holy estate that was instituted by God, not invented by men. If we are committed we should marry; if not, why are we together? This is not the way of today's society but it is still God's way! In marriage we are not afraid to give our word and sign our name. If we love each other we should be willing to declare that love openly through marriage.

Yet there does need to be a word of warning to the man who **runs off with another woman** or the woman who abandons her family. The difficulties and pain that your family experience are a direct result of your decision. Unless you come to repentance the decimation of their lives will be held to your account. You have abandoned a sacred trust and broken a vow made before God. Your healing is only possible through deep and swift repentance. Come to your senses before it is too late, before your heart is too hard to care? Remember the plain words of the Bible, *Prov 6:27 "Can a man scoop fire into his lap without his clothes being burned? So is he who sleeps with another man's wife; no-one who touches her will go unpunished."*

The future consummation. Rev 19:7, 21:2-4, 22:4-5, 17 + 20.

Now that we know we are called to be the bride of Christ, our task is to prepare for the wedding day.

God is seeking His bride; the bride's response is to prepare for the wedding. She is to prepare herself. He will come at an hour we do not expect, the Revelation announces this great day. *Rev 19:7, "Let us rejoice and be glad and give him glory! For the wedding of the Lamb has come, and his bride has made herself ready."*

Paul's call to the Church at Corinth was to become what they really were. He says, *"I promised you to one husband, to Christ, so that I might present you as a pure virgin to him. But I am afraid that just as Eve was deceived by the serpent's cunning, your minds may somehow be led astray from your sincere and pure devotion to Christ." 2 Cor 11:2-3.* The response of the bride is to be one of devotion and preparation.

Think of how a bride prepares for her wedding day, the dress is bought, the list is prepared, and the shoes are carefully chosen. If she is following tradition she wears something old, something new, something borrowed, and something blue, all this to please her husband. The venue is booked, the minister visited, the holiday confirmed, and many other details are joyfully sorted. In God's Kingdom, the groom will not look upon the outside but upon the heart. We must prepare our character if we are to stand before God without fault and with great joy. We can never merit the love of Christ, but we can respond to that love and aim to please Him. For our guide we have the word of God, the witness of the Spirit and the voice of conscience. If we walk against any of these we are ill prepared to meet the bridegroom.

It is only when the bride is finally ready, that we will reign with Him as God originally intended. God will have his partner throughout all eternity. *Rev 21:2-4 "I saw the Holy City, the new Jerusalem, coming down out of heaven from God, prepared as a bride beautifully dressed for her husband. And I heard a loud voice from the throne saying, "Now the dwelling of God is with men, and he will live with them. They will be his people, and God himself will be with them and be their God. He will wipe every tear from their eyes. There will be no more death or mourning or crying or pain, for the old order of things has passed away."*

Here the illustration gives way to reality. As Adam received Eve, someone comparable to himself, that he could share his love with, so God will receive His bride: someone made in His own image, suitable to her role, one who can rejoice in His love through all eternity. We are not simply going to heaven; we are going as the bride, to reign with Christ, to be the recipient of his love. In heaven we will meet the passionate God. *Rev 22:4-5 "they shall see his face; and his name shall be in their foreheads. -- And they shall reign for ever and ever. KJV*

A problem with submission?

In that new kingdom, the bride will be comparable to her husband, but still be in loving submission to Him. For just as the husband is said to be head of the wife, so we see Christ is the head of His Church. Eph 5:22-23. Again marriage is a visual aid, which grants us a glimpse of the relationship we will have with God in heaven. We will have no difficulty taking a submissive place to our heavenly bridegroom, His love will overwhelm us and we will be overjoyed to be chosen.

We must not misunderstand this mystery. In our fallen world, where leadership is bases on power not love, we will continue to have difficulties with headship. Christian headship is never domineering. In the Scripture, love is the only motivation for leadership. On earth leadership may be selfish or ineffectual, but in the new heaven and new earth, when we see God face to face, we will always want to live in submission to the one who died for us. His headship is perfect because it is based on perfect love. His love has been tested and proved by his selfless life and sacrificial death.

God created us to know only good and finally that purpose will be accomplished. Till then, *"each one of you also must love his wife as he loves himself, and the wife must respect her husband." Eph 5:33.* If couples determine to live in love and respect towards each other, they will find other problems are sorted out. God's model for marriage practical and it works!!!

Still seeking His Bride!

As Abraham's servant sought a bride for Isaac, (Gen 24) so the Spirit of God seeks the bride of Christ. In Genesis the servant sought the bride, bestowed gifts upon her and led her through the desert to the groom. In the same way, we are called of the Spirit and granted his gifts. He leads us through this barren world, but we are looking for the bride groom. The hymn writer said, "Unto Him who has loved us and washed us from sin, Unto Him be the glory forever. Amen."

This is our purpose and our hope; we were created to be the bride of Christ. The last words of the Bible take up this theme, *Rev 22:17+20 "the Spirit and the bride say, Come. And let him that heareth say, Come. And let him that is athirst come. And whosoever will, let him take the water of life freely. He who testifies to these things says; I am coming quickly.* **Amen.** - *Come, Lord Jesus."*

Important Questions.

1: Are you devoted to the well being of your partner?

2: What have you given up to gain a better marriage?

3: How does love prompt a response and draw the best out of your spouse?

4: Do you criticise or compliment?

5: Why does the Bible say God hates divorce?

(Remember though God hates divorce, he does not hate those who go through divorce.)

6: Have we sought forgiveness for our part in any divorce?

Remember do not speak idly about divorce; it plants seeds of doubt and undermines love. There is no such thing as an amicable divorce!

7: Are you committed to make it work even when things get tough?

8: Are you part of the Bride of Christ?

9: Are you preparing to meet Christ the heavenly Bridegroom?

10: Do you passionately love this passionate God?

A prayer for those who want to renew their marriage covenant.

Father God, thank you for my Husband / Wife. Forgive us where we have been selfish, angry or unconcerned about each other's needs. Help us to keep our vow to love each other even when everything seems to be against us. We humble ourselves before you now and ask that you will help us to put into operation those things that will enrich our marriage. We place each other in your hands and pray that you would restore and renew our love.

Father, we pledge again that we are committed to keeping our vows, grant us we pray kind and gentle hearts towards each other. Where we have sinned, we ask forgiveness; where we have been sinned against, help us forgive.

May we encourage not criticise. May we listen more than we seek to be heard, and may we be best friends. We give you our days Lord; they are in your hands; now guide us, as we go forwards in new hope together. For Christ's sake hear us, **Amen.**

God hears the prayer of those who are humble in heart, and he will show you how to act in love and commitment if you seek his help. Remember to talk together often and give your love the time it needs to grow strong.

A prayer for those who want to follow Christ.

Saviour of all, I confess that I have not followed you with a whole and undivided heart. Today I place my life in your hands and pray that you would forgive the sins of my past. Where I have lived for myself and ignored your ways, Father for Jesus sake, forgive me.

I acknowledge that Jesus died for my sins and I ask that by your Holy Spirit you would cleanse my heart and live in my life. Today I place my future in your control, lead me to a Church where I may learn of you and learn to serve you.

God of Heaven and earth, forgive my past, cleanse my present, and guide my future. May I be truly one of your people, a valued part of the bride of Christ!

Thank you that you love me with a passion and zeal, you have called me to follow you and today I am saying yes. I make this prayer in the name of Jesus Christ our Saviour and Lord, **Amen.**

For those who have decided to follow Christ, it is important now that you tell a Christian friend about your decision, and that you find a Church where you may learn more of what it means to follow Christ. If you have a Bible now is the time to begin to red it. Start with the life of Jesus, beginning at Luke's Gospel; if you read one chapter a day it will take three weeks to read through the life of Christ. Luke also wrote the book of Acts, which tells us what happened after Christ returned to Heaven. You should also talk to God about what you have read and how it can affect your life. Prayer is simply a conversation with God about His will for our lives, and His will is revealed through the Bible. May our Saviour Jesus guide your marriage and strengthen your faith till the day you see him face to face.

The Sex Chapter.

Prov 5:18-19 "May you rejoice in the wife of your youth. A loving doe, a graceful deer-- may her breasts satisfy you always, may you ever be captivated by her love."

Once we understand the frame work for sexual relationships, i.e. that it is meant to be the expression of the total commitment of two people who are covenanted to each within marriage; then we find that the Bible teaches that Sex was created to be a delight to both husband & wife. We need to remember that sex without commitment is deeply wounding to both parties whereas sex with commitment is deeply affirming.

Sex for the whole person.

To make a sexual relationship all it can be, a married couple needs to relate in all three areas of their being, body, soul & spirit. A marriage which has lost its joy will soon loose its sexual lustre. While we live on earth our primary experiences are through our bodies. God created us as sexual beings, and if that sexual dimension is unduly denied, within a marriage, then it will create both tension & temptation. St Paul is clear about this, *1 Cor 7:5 "Do not refuse one another except perhaps by agreement for a season, that you may devote yourselves to prayer; but then come together again, lest Satan tempt you through lack of self-control." RSV*

In Spirit we are united when we share the one goal, a life lived to the glory of God. A shared faith & a shared prayer life will deepen our spiritual union. Our souls unite when we support each other in our feelings, our desires & our emotions. Making love may only be a small part of any day but it is prepared for in the 24 hours that lead up to that moment. We need to be the best friend & greatest encourager of our partner. Physically we are united when we join together in the act of making love. Here, the *"two shall be one flesh"*. Which the

Bible calls, *"a great mystery: Eph 5:31-32."*
However because our body is linked through mind & heart to our soul & the soul is the realm where the spirit expresses itself, a bad sexual relationship will affect our soul, (our feelings & emotions) which will in turn affect our spirit.

This is why Paul warns us against prostitution, uniting ourselves to a prostitute is a sure way of polluting both soul & spirit. He writes, *1 Cor 6:15-19"Shall I then take the members of Christ, (My body) and make them the members of a harlot? God forbid. -- Know ye not that he which is joined to a harlot is one body (with her)? For two, -- shall be one flesh. But he that is joined unto the Lord is one spirit (with him). Flee fornication. --- He that commitments fornication sinneth against his own body. --- Your body is the temple of the Holy Ghost which is in you, which ye have of God." KJV*

Sex before marriage is "fornication", sex outside marriage is "adultery," and the scripture is very clear: God will judge both the fornicator and the adulterer.

Love, not sex.

People in love are called to be lovers. Sex without love is no more than an animal emotion; sex with love is God's desire for all married couples. This is why we call it making love. Sex without love is incomplete, but sex as an expression of love is blessed by God. Sex in the Bible is seen as the culmination of our commitment, and not as the convenience of a casual relationship. It is the consummation of a relationship; not he commencement of one. This chapter aims to make some practical suggestions, based on Biblical principles for improving your love life.

Now, the Bible could never be seen as a sex manual, however it is a book about relationships, primarily the relationship between God & mankind, but then also nations & individual people. Which means it is not silent on this most intimate of relationships. *Song 7:7-8 "Thy stature is like to a palm-tree, and thy breasts to its clusters. I said, I will climb up into the palm-tree, I will take hold of the branches thereof: Let thy breasts be as clusters of the vine, And the smell of thy breath like apples. ASV"*

If we are to follow the recipe for married life given in scripture this means we can never bow to the pressures of society and excuse ourselves for indulging in promiscuity. A biblical sexual relationship is heterosexual, monogamous and joyous. A Christian husband is called to satisfy his wife and a Christian wife is called to satisfy her husband. For those who hold a shared faith this satisfaction should enter into the deepest level of their personality.

Sex itself takes place on three levels, it may be physical, psychological and spiritual; in other words the act of intercourse is meant to affect the whole person, body, soul & spirit. Many times couples miss out on all they could share by simply functioning on the physical or biological level. Here sex is seen as an urge to be satisfied, there may be no more commitment to sex than personal gratification. The TV and movies display this casual relationship as the most desirable of all, "sex with a stranger", no commitments and no consequences. However, that isn't even true in Hollywood, just look at the lives of the stars. If this attitude enters into marriage it can be deeply destructive. Sex especially for the wife must be more than a release; it must be the culminating act of a loving relationship. We cannot ignore each other all day & then expect a rapturous experience in the bedroom.

Try a little tenderness.

Many marriages grow cold because lovemaking becomes lazy. Remember, "If a thing is worth doing it is worth doing well." This is doubly true of making love. Even the Bible hints at possible preparations. It suggests atmosphere, anticipation, scent & sight are all important. *Prov 7:16-18* a woman seeks to tempt a man saying, *"I have decked my bed with coverings of tapestry, with carved works, with fine linen of Egypt. I have perfumed my bed with myrrh, aloes, and cinnamon. Come; let us take our fill of love." KJV.* Scent and sight were the back drop to her temptation, but when the same details are incorporated in a marriage, it is no longer a temptation but a gift of love. The book of the Song of Solomon also paints a picture of the preparation & desire for love. *Song 5:1"I am come into my garden, my sister, my spouse: I have gathered my myrrh with my spice; I have eaten my honeycomb with my honey; I have drunk my wine with my milk: --I have put off my coat -- have washed my feet; --My beloved put in his hand by the (handle) of the door, and my (Heart) moved for him. KJV updated.*

Preparation is important; for the wife it creates an emotional climate which is conducive to love. This may involve music, candles, or perfume and appropriate clothing. To make love well certainly needs privacy, with no distractions from any children. It also means making love a priority and not leaving it to the very end of the day when only the dregs of time and energy are left.

The Bible not only speaks of creating the right atmosphere but of what we would call foreplay. Let us not forget the humble kiss as we begin to express love for each other, in scripture, the bride says to the husband, *"Let him kiss me with the kisses of his mouth: for thy love is better than wine. Songs 1:2.* The couple then move on to touch, *"His left arm is under my head, and his right arm embraces me." Song 2:6.* Here we can see that the lover is on the right side of his beloved, as they lie together he supports her with his left hand & caresses her with his right. We should not rush into making love but build slowly towards the loving act. In this context the man has been compared to a gas cooker which comes to life quickly & roars away merrily, but can be extinguished just as quickly, while the woman has been compared to a pressure cooker, to get the best results we need to build the pressure slowly so that everything comes to the boil at the same time.

Giving and receiving.

This means, when making love, we need to be aware of our partner's needs; our first aim is to give them pleasure not to receive self gratification. We should not take pleasure but give pleasure, and when each lover concentrates on the other both will be satisfied. For if we are seeking to satisfy our partner, we will in turn find satisfaction. When we make love properly then we enter into the world of the soul. We are not just engaging with each other physically but emotionally. Making love must proclaim to our partner, that they are the most precious person in our lives and that we want to share the most intimate part of ourselves with them and no one else. When we make love we are emotionally vulnerable, there is nakedness of soul as well as of body, so love must be an act of trust & kindness. Abuse occurs when Sex is forced against the feelings of the other. There must be no exploitation or domination in the act of love. The bedroom is not the place to act out fantasies but to please our partner.

So our first goal in lovemaking must be to give pleasure to our partner. The man must aim to please his wife, and the wife to please her husband. If we are trying to take pleasure rather than give pleasure, one partner may be satisfied & the other deeply wounded. If our aim is to give pleasure to each other then the relationship will be strengthened & enriched. But do remember not every act of lovemaking will be an earth moving experience; tiredness, preparation & health all play a part, if we are dog tired, and 11-00 pm has come and gone, we will be unlikely to experience all that we could in making love. We have given our strength to other things and made love a low priority.

Beware the danger hour!

It would also be wise to go to bed together. If one stays

downstairs watching the TV and the other goes to bed, two dangers are present. Firstly the one in bed on their own will begin to question how much they are loved, and second, the one watching TV may be tempted to watch late night pornography. This is a real temptation for some men and needs to be resisted by making each other a priority. Pornography profanes the act of love; it provides biological sex without either tenderness or intimacy. It promises instant pleasure but can destroy relationships. Firstly it will create guilt & come between husband and wife. Then it will de-sensitize the watcher to wholesome lovemaking. It actually produces impotency, because greater stimuli are needed to get the same response, and all the time the watcher is becoming cold to the one he has wowed to love. Then, it introduces the danger of comparison. Someone watching pornography will finally compare their experience of their partner to the lie they are watching on TV. This is a most dangerous area. It is highly addictive, it makes liars of men, for they try to deceive their wives, it breaks marriages & it DOES NOT SATISFY.

There is hope, but only through genuine repentance. We must change our attitude and not only our actions. We must in sincerity confess our sins to God, we cannot make excuses, sin is always a choice, and we must confess that we chose to follow temptation. No-one is immune and we all need to heed the warning of the Bible, *"let him that thinks he stands take heed lest he fall. There hath no temptation taken you but such as is common to man: but God is faithful, who will not suffer you to be tempted above that ye are able; but will with the temptation also make a way to escape, 1 Cor 10:12-13* KJV. The only hope is to confess this sin and ask God's forgiveness.

Next we will need to be open with our partner and ask their forgiveness. They need to know we love them, and not some sexual fantasy we are indulging in. Then sorrow must be shown in more than words; we must take steps to avoid the danger. The same danger exists with the internet. If something has to be done in secret then it is probably a sin, if it causes us to love in deception and lies, it will take us from God & estrange us from our partner. Jesus said, *"That whosoever looks on a woman to lust after her hath committed adultery with her already in his heart."* Matt 5:28 KJV. We cannot have a heart full of adultery and expect to follow Jesus Christ. Paul tells us that love *"does not delight in evil"* 1 Cor 13, so we must take his advice to Timothy and *"Flee - youthful lusts: but follow righteousness, faith, (Love and), peace."* 2 Tim 2:22 KJV.

We need as Bob Dylan wrote to, "change our way of thinking get ourselves a different set of rules, put our best foot forward and stop being influenced by fools." Immorality must become unattractive, we must see it in its ugliness, & loving our partner must become our chief goal.

We also need to forgive each other. We cannot hold a grudge. If our partner comes in humility to confess their sin, then our faith must rise to forgiveness and seek to help them defeat temptation. We are not the judge, God is, and where He forgives we must follow. Remember Jesus' words about forgiveness, *"if he trespasses against thee seven times in a day, and seven times in a day turn again to thee, saying, I repent; thou shalt forgive him."* Luke 17:4. However we must not use forgiveness as an excuse for immoral actions. We are called to forgive when someone confesses their fault, but we will only be able to fully trust them again when they prove they are trustworthy. Forgiveness must come in a moment of time; trust is built up over a period of time, as the penitent person proves their change of heart and mind.

This may take some time because once we form a habit it is a track which our mind automatically follows unthinkingly, like a sheep to slaughter. We actually need to fill our mind with good things, we need to spend time together, romance each other and renew our love. We need to read what the Bible says on love and marriage, and read other Christian books on marriage. Sharing the prayers and questions in this book is a good start. The Bible tells us how to change, *"be - transformed by the renewing of your mind."* *Rom 12:2*, it is up to us to put that change into practice, by changing our thought patterns. One good practice is to Go to Bed Together and so avoid temptation!!! Pornography is a trap set to destroy your marriage. *Prov 7:21-23 "With -- fair speech she caused him to yield, with the flattering of her lips she forced him. He goeth after her straightway, as an ox goeth to the slaughter, or as a fool to the -- stocks; Till a dart strike through his liver; as a bird hastens to the snare, - knowing not that it is - his life (he will loose). KJV updated.*

Sex is not the same as love and pornography is an affront to genuine lovemaking. It values the experience above the person. The participants become no more than meat for our pleasure. We need to run form its pollution and make love with pure hearts. If each one feels valued and lovemaking affirms how important you are to your partner, then both husband & wife will be keen to enjoy each other & experiment in the bedroom.

Vive la difference!

Perhaps we should recognize that men and women have a basically different attitude to sex. At night after a long day when the wife goes to bed, the first thought on her mind is probably sleep. But the husband is stimulated by sight, and so as his wife prepares for bed, a glimpse of her body may be all it takes for him to be ready for love. This can make the wife think all he is interested in is sex, this is not really true. It is just that the male is designed to be stimulated by the sight of a woman.

This means that the husband will often be the initiator in the act of love. This may not always be so for there are times in the month when a woman's natural cycle makes her more amorous than others, but as a rule it will probably be the man who initiates & the woman who responds. This is an important moment, which can be so easily misunderstood. Often the man can assume that his wife is as interested in making love as he is, then when she fails to respond immediately he feels rejected. To the wife the husband's keenness can seem domineering; she may feel he is only interested in her body. She may well feel that with little or no warning she is asked to light up like a Christmas tree, solely for his pleasure & gratification. The husband needs to remember to woo his wife and the wife needs to remember to welcome her husband.

Here we are dealing with one of the psychological differences of men & women. A man is visually stimulated, the abundance of pornographic literature testifies to this. A woman is far more likely to respond to loving tenderness & a genuine concern for her. If the husband arrives home, falls asleep in front of the TV & does not take any interest in his wife's day, he is destroying his own sex life. 1 *Peter 3:7 "husbands, -- live with your wives in an understanding way, --- and show her honour as a fellow heir of the grace of life." NASU.* If the husband spends time with his wife, listens to her thoughts and lets her recount her day, she will feel supported, and then she will genuinely feel more disposed to making love. His interest in his wife must be on this level of the soul, she must know that she is more important then the job or the TV or the hobby. She must know that she is more than an attractive body to him; but someone he values and cherishes. If she comes first in his heart & he shows it in his actions, then the bedroom will blossom.

Think of how keen a young man is to please his girlfriend when they are courting. That same spirit of devotion needs to be continued throughout the marriage. If we will invest time in each other, if we will treat each other with respect and love then the flame of passion can soon be re-ignited. Remember your vow and don't give up.

If you want to enjoy good sex then don't be a lazy lover. If a wife wants to encourage her husband, she should realise how important the right clothing is. We all dress up to go to a party or a meal. Since a man is stimulated visually a wife can dress to encourage her partner. Provocative (sexy) clothing is quite acceptable when given as a gift of love. It is the promise of things to come, it is the joy of delighting our partner, and it is the delight of the husband's eyes. As the husband in Solomon's song looks at his beloved, he sees her dressed in a veil and decked with a necklace, her beauty is his delight, and his desire is aroused. *"Your lips are like a strand of scarlet, and your mouth is lovely. Your temples behind your veil are like a piece of pomegranate. Your neck is like the tower of David, Built for an armoury, on which hang a thousand bucklers, all shields of mighty men. Your two breasts are like two fawns, Twins of a gazelle, which feed among the lilies." Song 4:3-5 NKJV*

How we dress will inevitably provoke a response, what the young woman knows when she is seeking a partner the wife should remember when she is with her husband. Sight stimulates a husband's love.

One other thing may help: simple cleanliness can also go a long way to helping in the bedroom. Strangely most women do not appreciate the smell of a men sweat, nor do they like a stubbly beard! We can if we are wise shower or shave before bed! We should certainly make sure our teeth are clean and our breath is sweet. Dragons' breath will wither the hottest ardour. Again the Song of Solomon speaks to us, *"Let now your breasts be like clusters of the vine, the fragrance of your breath like apples, and the roof of your mouth like the best wine." Song 7:8-9 NKJV*

A helping hand!

A younger man will find little difficulty with becoming aroused; but a man in his middle years will often find that his spirit is willing but his flesh is not. He retains the desire but not the performance. His body may not be immediately responsive, so his wife's caresses can be very helpful. He does not need belittling, nor should a couple panic, and think that their sex life is over. What he needs is encouraging; he needs a wife's helping hand. When the strength of youth is passing, a couple can still enjoy a good sex life if they learn to put a few simple steps in place.

Things like eating well, regular exercise, going to bed early; (not expecting to be full of energy after 11-00 or even sometimes after10-00 pm) will all help. It will help to spend time together before the bedroom starts, undressing each other, and taking time to concentrate on each other in foreplay. The important thing is to communicate. Tell each other what works and what doesn't work, and above all concentrate on what you are doing. Being present in body but absent in spirit, will soon cause difficulties. Be willing to laugh together and be glad when things go well, but don't worry too much when they don't. Your aim is not a virtuoso performance but to satisfy your partner, if you do that then love making is a success.

You are what you eat!

We need to listen to our bodies, and what we eat can affect our sex life. Some supplements may help, L-Arginine, (an amino acid) or Avena Sativa (an extract from green oats) can have a positive affect on the male libido, while the herb Damiana or the Kava kava root, (A herbal muscle relaxant) can have a beneficial affects on women in their mid years. Tofu (soy bean curd) & Tempeh eaten regularly are also recommended for the menopause, as is the herb, black cohosh. The Herb Saw Palmetto is recommended for men in their middle years with prostate problems. However, before taking any of these supplements I would recommend further reading and research into their nature and function. This is just a starting point for further research. Viagra is certainly not the only way to go. On a general health level, drinking tea not coffee, especially green tea can be good for the blood; the main antioxidant in green tea is 200 times stronger than vitamin E and 500 times more than vitamin C. It will aid in detoxifying of the body.

It would seem to me that if we want to enjoy a long and enriching sex life there are a few simple rules.

- Spend time together outside the bedroom. (An occasional meal out, a walk together or a weekend away will enrich any relationship)
- Listen to each other, in and out of the bedroom.
- Remember your primary aim is to satisfy your partner, so encourage each other.
- Make love a priority by retiring for the night together. (If you have children take advantage of the times when they are not around, be innovative.)
- Don't rush into love making; work on the mood and the atmospheres.
- Give time to kissing and caressing, talk about what works and what does not.
- Encourage and affirm your partner, remember a woman is responsive to tenderness and needs to know she is more than a sex object; a man is stimulated by sight and touch.
- Beware of temptations. Take every step to avoid pornography, it is very damaging.
- Take a little exercise, a daily walk can be very helpful, & watch what you eat.
- Never talk about divorce, but work on strengthening your relationship.
- Remember; you were created to relate in three areas body, soul and spirit.

A Prayer.

Lord, you have made us passionate people, Thank you for this great gift, help us to keep ourselves pure and make us a blessing to each other as we share the wonderful gift of love. Since you made us to love, grant us the wisdom to love in the way you intended. AMEN.

Beating the Adultery epidemic!

Ex 20:14: "You shall not commit adultery" NKJV

Old Testament: - Proverbs 6:32 + Lev 20:10. N
New Testament Heb 13:4, Matthew 5:27-28.

Selfish commands & protective commandments.
1. God invented Sex. Gen 2:23-25.
2. He is against the Misuse of Sex.

The danger of uncontrolled passion.
(David & Bathsheba: 2Sam 11:1-27.)
Adultery is never a single sin.

1. He was in the wrong place at the wrong time. 2Sam 11:1
2. He played with temptation. Mt 5:28.
3. He was tempted by a spiritual person.
4. He covered up with murder deceit and lies.

How to protect our marriages.

1. Don't stray into the wrong place.
2. Don't play with temptation. Acts 19:19.
3. Strengthen your marriage. *Rev 2:5*
4. Get close to God.
5. Repent and find help. John 8:1-11.
6. Honour faithfulness. We live by different standards.

God means what He says.
- In Judgement. 1Cor 6:9-11.
- In forgiveness. 2Cor 5:17. John 8:11

Beating the Adultery epidemic!

Ex 20:14, "You shall not commit adultery." NKJV is possibly the least respected of the 10 Commandments in society. We understand that adultery is wrong in principle, but today it is the subject of jokes and paraded freely as entertainment on TV. We live in a society which thinks little of sex before marriage, and only feigns an outcry, when public figures are found to be as frail and corruptible as everyone else. Bill Clinton becomes a by word for immorality, but we hardly raise an eyebrow when John Major is found to have had an affair with Edwina Curry.

Sex is glamorised today as never before. It is used to sell, to shock, and to entertain. TV advertising, soaps and Hollywood films drip with sexual, plots from the vulgar to the seductive. Everything is available from reality TV romps, to late night explicit movies, and the internet is even worse. Our grand parents would not believe what we watch today in the name of entertainment. We excuse it, because it is behind closed doors and between consenting adults. It doesn't hurt anyone, does it? This commandment seems strangely out of step with the overwhelming direction of modern day society.

Yet the Bible is clear. *Ex 20:14, "You shall not commit adultery."*

Proverbs 6:32, tells us why, *"whoever commits adultery with a woman lacks understanding; He who does so destroys his own soul."* And the Old Testament punishment is severe. *Lev 20:10, "he who commits adultery with his neighbour's wife, the adulterer and the adulteress, shall surely be put to death." NKJV*

The New Testament is no less convinced about the need for faithfulness. *Heb 13:4, "Marriage should be honoured by all, and the marriage bed kept pure, for God will judge the adulterer and all the sexually immoral."*

Jesus went further, *"Matt 5:27-28 "You have heard that it was said ---, "Thou shalt not commit adultery": But I say unto you, that who ever looks on a woman to lust after her has committed adultery with her already in his heart."* (KJV modernised)

Have you noticed how, when ever we are told not to do something, we automatically react against it! Something in human nature does not want to be told what to do. We feel our freedom is being stifled. Surely this is a biological urge like eating or drinking, therefore it is to be acted upon. So we reduce ourselves to the level of the animals, and even act as an animal would.

(The difference between men and animals is profound! We were created in the "Image of God" (Gen 1:26), the human being is a three part being, Body, soul and Spirit. We are different to the plants, a Tree has a body, but it is not made in God's image it has no soul. We are separated from the animals, an animal has a body and soul, but it is not made in God's image, as it has no spirit. Only mankind has body, soul and spirit. By allowing our spiritual side and our rational side to be pre-eminent we are able to control our biological side.)

Man is not just a physical and biological creature, we are spiritual beings, living souls and what we do with our bodies affects both soul and spirit, so *"whoever commits adultery---destroys his own soul." Prov 6:32.*

This sis why God gives us a commandment in this area! There are two kinds of commandment, one for the good of the speaker, "bring me my slippers, or pass the marmalade!" The other is for the good of the one who receives it. At the end of the dock the sign says STOP. If we ignore it we will wreck our car and perhaps wreck our lives. We are told not to commit adultery because it is bad for us. To drive past this sign is self destructive.

The Bible is not prudish or unrealistic about sex. It speaks very honestly about sex; God invented it to be the crowning glory of a couple's relationship together. One of the first commandments given to mankind was be fruitful and multiply, and you can not do that outside of sex.

The first act Adam is asked to perform following his creation was to name all the animals. The result is, that he finds that for every creature there is a mate, except for him; and God says, *"It is not good for a man to be alone."* Something has awakened in Adam; he has become aware of his need of a partner of the opposite sex. Then Eve is brought to him and Adam rejoices, in her creation, he is even inspired to write a love poem, *Gen 2:23, "This is now bone of my bones, and flesh of my flesh: she shall be called Woman, because she was taken out of Man." KJV.*

The next verse introduces us to the concept of marriage, *"therefore shall a man leave his father and his mother, and shall cleave unto his wife: and they shall be one flesh. And they were both naked, the man and his wife, and were not ashamed. Gen 2:24-25. KJV.* Here we actually have the prototype for marriage. In a Biblical marriage, a new family is created; they *"leave their father and mother"*. A mutual and exclusive commitment is made, they *"cleave to one another"*. And the act of sex is celebrated, as *"the two become one flesh"*: So marriage is introduced as an exclusive union between a man and a woman, which is publicly proclaimed, permanent sealed and privately celebrated." Marriage is the original place to celebrate our sexual nature.

It is the misuse of sex which the Bible is concerned about. Sex is seen as a precious gift, and all precious gifts are to be handled with care. The Best dinner plate or the best china coffee set is handled with care. There is a vulnerability between two people who make love, they are not only joined to each other physically but emotionally and when under God's blessing spiritually. If there is no commitment, then physical union can be deeply damaging.

If we don't think sex can be damaging ask the teenage girl who falls pregnant after a one night stand, ask the child who grows up without a father, because all he wanted was a quick thrill. Ask the cotenant of Africa as it struggles with the Aids Pandemic, spread through casual sex. Ask the wife or husband who are shattered by their partner infidelity, and ask the children as they greave the loss of a parent and try to understand why?

The Bible gives us a classic example of a Good man falling into adultery and there are many warnings in it for us today. It is the account of David and Bathsheba.

2 Sam 11v1-27. "At the time when kings go forth to battle, - David sent Joab, and his servants with him, and all Israel; and they destroyed the children of Ammon, and besieged Rabbah. But David tarried - at Jerusalem. – In the evening, David arose from - his bed, and walked upon the roof of the king's house: from the roof he saw a woman washing herself; and the woman was very beautiful. And David - inquired after the woman. And one said, Is not this Bath-Sheba, the daughter of Eliam, the wife of Uriah the Hittite? And David sent messengers, and took her; and she came to him, and he lay with her; for she was purified from her uncleanness: and she returned unto her house.

And the woman conceived, and - told David, - "I am with child." David sent to Joab, saying, Send me Uriah the Hittite. And when Uriah was come --, David asked -- how Joab did, and how the war prospered. Then David said to Uriah, Go down to thy house, and wash thy feet. And Uriah departed, --- But slept at the door of the king's house with all the servants --

and went not down to his house. When they told David, "Uriah went not down unto his house," David said to Uriah, -- why - did you not go down to your house? And Uriah said "The ark, and Israel, and Judah, abide in tents; and my lord Joab, and the servants of my lord, are encamped in the open fields; shall I then go to my house, to eat and to drink, and to lie with my wife? As you live, and as your soul lives, I will not do this thing." David said to Uriah, Tarry here to day also, and tomorrow I will let thee depart. So Uriah abode in Jerusalem. And when David called him, he ate and drank; and David made him drunk: and at evening he went out to lie on his bed with the servants of his lord, but went not down to his house. -- In the morning, David wrote a letter to Joab, and sent it by the hand of Uriah. He wrote "Set - Uriah in the forefront of the hottest battle, and retire - from him, that he may die." And – Joab - assigned Uriah to a place where he knew that valiant men were. The men of the city went out, and fought with Joab: and some fell; and Uriah the Hittite also died. Then Joab -- told David; -- So the messenger went, -- and showed David all that Joab had sent him for. (He reported) some of the king's servants are dead, and your servant Uriah the Hittite is dead also. -- And when the wife of Uriah heard that Uriah her husband was dead, she mourned for her husband. And when the time of mourning was past, David -- fetched her to his house, and she became his wife, and bore him a son. But the thing that David had done displeased the LORD. (KJV modernised)

The Adultery is not the only sin David commits, one sin leads to another; adultery is followed by embarrassment, fear, lies, scheming and murder & theft. The world tells us that there are no consequences to casual sex. In a world of aids and broken lives are we so foolish as to believe there are no consequences?

There are many warnings here. The first is how destructive the force of lust is when it is let loose. If this story were not in the Bible, but came from some other source about the Great King

David, we would never believe it! David the Sweet singer of Israel, the composer of Psalms, The anointed King of God's people, the man after God's own heart, is an adulterer?

This is a warning about our frailty, the steps to his downfall are obvious but many walk them today.

1.   **He opened himself to temptation.** He was in "The wrong place the wrong time." *"At the time **when kings go forth to battle**, that David **sent Joab**." 2Sam 11:1.* When we are at ease, sitting back we are most vulnerable. We can open ourselves to temptations at work. The office romance begins by saying, "my wife doesn't understand me like you do." My husband doesn't listen to me, but you really understand how I am feeling." A coffee break away from work, a lunch together and we are in the wrong place at the wrong time, temptations can come, if we put ourselves in compromising situations. If we find ourselves thinking about sex with another person we are in a dangerous place, Adultery is in our heart, and what is in our heart, we may finally act upon. Remember even the act of imagining adultery is a sin which needs confessing to find forgiveness.

2.   **He played with temptation.** On the roof, he looked again and again. It is not the first look that kills it is the second. Adultery begins in the heart. That is why Jesus said, *"Anyone who even looks at a woman with lust in his eye has already committed adultery with her in his heart". Matt 5:28 TLB.* Then he asked her name, the lust is growing! He may rationalise it, well this was just curiosity, and he should know who his subjects are! Remember to rationalise is just to tell ourselves rational-lies. By the time he sends for her, before she enters the room the deed is already unstoppable. You need to stop before the bedroom door or it is too late.

If David could be tempted we can certainly be tempted. Sexual temptation is more addictive and more powerful than almost any other temptation. Men in particular are strongly drawn to the physical form of the opposite sex. If we indulge that temptation it will become a dominating feature in our lives. The power of sex is well understood by people wanting to make money, advertising, TV, Web sights and films are full of sex just because it is so powerfully attractive to us.

3.   **He was tempted by a spiritual person.** Ritual of washing was a Jewish purification ritual. A believer will rarely be tempted by a brash none believer but someone who seems to understand and appreciate them. Beware! Sex has destroyed priests and politicians. Kings and pop stars have been destroyed by their un-bridled sex lives. It has destroyed stronger people that us so we must take its power very seriously.

4.   **It was followed by cover up and deceit.** He may have expected one night of joy and that would be it. There are always consequences to sin. Some are obvious some are not; I have never known anyone caught in adultery where people were not deeply hurt. The idea of a bit of fun is a lie. There is no fun at all in the pain it causes afterwards. One sin will lead to another till there seems to be no way out and even the person who thought they were enjoying themselves will bed up full of guilt and deeply depressed or distressed. The **deception at home** will certainly ruin the closeness in the family relationship. No longer naked an un-ashamed!

What can we do?

1.   Don't be where you should not be. Would I do this or say this if my wife were here now?
2.   Don't play with temptation. Books TV, Acts19?
3.   Spend time strengthening your marriage. Marriage books & videos, 1 ½ hours a week. Day a month, meal out. Friendship is so important. Talk together; be open and

vulnerable to each other, listen and support each other. Why did David no God to his wife?

4.   Get close to God. The Heart of God is against adultery. Remember the guilt.

5.   Repent and find help. God offers forgiveness. Jn 8:1-11. Don't be judgemental.

6.   Do not be embarrassed to be faithful. Who is in control, body, emotions feelings and society, or Spirit?

We live in a world where the Bible's standards of faithfulness and commitment are viewed as repressive. Yet people are wounded every day by unfaithful partners.

STD, Daniel Low-Beer of Cambridge University told a group of MPs at the House of Commons that neglecting abstinence has led to a "crisis in sexually transmitted diseases". Rates of Chlamydia had risen 139 per cent in 5 years, syphilis had soared by 870 per cent and gonorrhoea cases had risen 67 per cent in women. Dr Low-Beer cited the Ugandan Aids and STD prevention scheme where teaching on abstinence and faithfulness in marriage had reduced casual sex by 65 per cent and HIV cases by 21 per cent. "Abstinence program's in the US had led to a drop of 7 per cent in casual sex and delayed sexual relations from age 15 to 17. Faithfulness in marriage and chastity before marriage works.

Sex can not be treated casually nor can God's word. He has not changed His mind; we have moved God has not. Today faithfulness is unusual; Bible standards are regarded with shock, scorn or disbelief. As Christians We are flowing against the tide in society; sadly this tide is carrying all kinds of destructive filth. God's word has not changed and he means what He says, *1 Cor 6:9-11 "Do you not know that the wicked will not inherit the kingdom of God? Do not be deceived: Neither the sexually immoral nor idolaters nor adulterers nor male prostitutes nor homosexual offenders nor thieves nor the greedy nor drunkards nor slanderers nor swindlers will inherit the kingdom of God."* The word of grace is, *"And that is what some of you were"*. God is not what seeking to judge us for our past if we will come in repentance and faithfulness to him. He want s to make us new people in Christ, *2 Cor 5:17 "if anyone is in Christ, he is a new creation; old things have passed away; behold, all things have become new."* If we have sinned and come in repentance to Christ we will find forgiveness and a new start. Only the new must "Go and sin no more." John 8.

A prayer

Father where we have sinned forgive us, when we are tempted keep us, where our love has grown cold give us the wisdom to renew our vows. We ask you to keep us faithful to each other and pray that our love will deepen over the years, this we ask through Jesus our saviour. Thank you for my Husband / Wife. Amen.

Marriage, The Bible Speaks.

21 Commonly asked Questions.

1. Is it OK to be single?
2. What about Divorce?
3. Does the Bible always say divorce is wrong?
4. What about separation?
5. What if my partner doesn't believe in God?
6. What if my partner dies?
7. Should a believer only marry a Christian?
8. What about adultery?
9. What about virginity?
10. What about immorality?
11. What about prostitution?
12. Should I return to my first partner?
13. What about forgiveness?
14. Who may enjoy sex?
15. Does the Bible really say we should enjoy sex?
16. How do I renew a faltering marriage?
17. What about children?
18. How to treat each other?
19. Is marriage for life?
20. Is Polygamy acceptable?
21. Who are these teachings for?

Marriage, the Bible speaks.

21 Commonly asked Questions.

There are many questions which the Bible does not answer; it doesn't tell us where to live, who we should marry, or what career to consider. But there are many questions the Bible does answer. In this chapter we let the Bible speak directly. The answers may not be popular but have stood the test of time; they provide the basis for a Christian family and may even promote a better love life. When we reinterpret Scripture, we must be very careful not to distort its plain meaning through our own prejudice. On moral issues we will find that the Bible says what it means and means what it says. It speaks plainly about both sin & forgiveness.

1. **Is it OK to be single?** Yes singleness is a gift from God. *1 Cor 7:7-9 "Each man has his own gift from God; one has this gift, another has that. Now to the unmarried and the widows I say: It is good for them to stay unmarried, as I am. But if they cannot control themselves, they should marry, for it is better to marry than to burn with passion."* Both marriage and singleness are gifts from God, we should celebrate both. The test is whether we can control our passions.

2. **What about divorce?** *Mal 2:14-16 "You have broken faith with, --- the wife of your marriage covenant. Has not [the LORD] made them one? In flesh and spirit they are his. --- So guard yourself in your spirit, and do not break faith with the wife of your youth. "I hate divorce," says the LORD God of Israel, -- So guard yourself in your spirit, and do not break faith."*

3. Does the Bible say divorce is always wrong? No, the Bible allows divorce in certain limited circumstances.

> *Matt 19:3-9 "Some Pharisees --- asked, "Is it lawful for a man to divorce his wife for any and every reason?" "Haven't you read," (Jesus) replied, "that at the beginning the Creator 'made them male and female', and said, 'For this reason a man will leave his father and mother and be united to his wife, and the two will become one flesh'? So they are no longer two, but one. Therefore what God has joined together, let man not separate." "Why then," they asked, "did Moses command that a man give his wife a certificate of divorce and send her away?" Jesus replied, "Moses permitted you to divorce your wives because your hearts were hard. But it was not this way from the beginning. I tell you that anyone who divorces his wife,* **except for marital unfaithfulness**, *and marries another woman commits adultery."*

I also believe David's prayer against a violent partner would apply in marriage, *Ps 140:1 "Deliver me, O LORD, from evil men; Preserve me from violent men." KJV*

4. Are these the only circumstances where people may separate? Paul tells us that separation is never God's best will; but if it does happen we can choose to be celibate.

> *1 Cor 7:10-11 "To the married I give this command (not I, but the Lord): A wife must not separate from her husband. But if she does, she must remain unmarried or else be reconciled to her husband. And a husband must not divorce his wife."* The same rule would apply to men.

5. Should I leave a partner who does not believe in God? No! You must keep your marriage vow and by living a Godly life seek to win your partner. *1 Cor 7:12-13 "If any brother has a wife who is not a believer and she is willing to live with him, he must not divorce her. And if a woman has a husband who is not a believer and he is willing to live with her, she must not divorce him."*

1 Peter 3:1-5 "Wives, in the same way be submissive to your husbands so that, if any of them do not believe the word, they may be won over without words by the behaviour of their wives, when they see the purity and reverence of your lives. Your beauty should not come from outward adornment, such as braided hair and the wearing of gold jewellery and fine clothes. Instead, it should be that of your inner self, the unfading beauty of a gentle and quiet spirit, which is of great worth in God's sight."

6. **What if a husband or wife dies, may we remarry**? **Yes!** *1 Cor 7:39 "A woman is bound to her husband as long as he lives. But if her husband dies, she is free to marry anyone she wishes, but he must belong to the Lord."*

7. **Should I marry someone who does not believe?** *2 Cor 6:14-16 "Do not be yoked together with unbelievers. For what do righteousness and wickedness have in common? Or what fellowship can light have with darkness? What does a believer have in common with an unbeliever?"* If families are divided on faith it will always cause tension.

8. **What does the Bible say about adultery?** *Prov 6:32-35 "A man who commits adultery lacks judgment; whoever does so destroys himself. Blows and disgrace are his lot, and his shame will never be wiped away; for jealousy arouses a husband's fury, and he will show no mercy when he takes revenge. He will not accept any compensation; he will refuse the bribe, however great it is."*

Ex 20:14 "Thou shalt not commit adultery. KJV

Heb 13:4 "Marriage should be honoured by all, and the marriage bed kept pure, for God will judge the adulterer and all the sexually immoral."

1 Cor 6:9-10 "The wicked will not inherit the kingdom of God? Do not be deceived: Neither the sexually immoral nor idolaters nor adulterers nor male prostitutes nor homosexual offenders nor thieves nor the greedy nor drunkards nor slanderers nor swindlers will inherit the kingdom of God."

9. **Does the Bible really expect people to be virgins when they marry?** Yes! To lose your virginity before marriage was a great slur on your character. To be falsely accused of immorality was very serious.

Deut 22:13-18 "If a man takes a wife and, after lying with her, dislikes her and slanders her and gives her a bad name, saying, "I married this woman, but when I approached her, I did not find proof of her virginity," then the girl's father and mother shall bring proof that she was a virgin to the town elders at the gate. The girl's father will say to the elders, "I gave my daughter in marriage to this man, but he dislikes her. Now he has slandered her and said, 'I did not find your daughter to be a virgin.' But here is the proof of my daughter's virginity." Then her parents shall display the cloth before the elders of the town, and the elders shall take the man and punish him."

Remember that Joseph nearly divorced Mary because he thought she had been immoral.

Matt 1:18-20 "Mary was pledged to be married to Joseph, but before they came together, she was found to be with child through the Holy Spirit. Because Joseph her husband was a righteous man and did not want to expose her to public disgrace, he had in mind to divorce her quietly. But after he had considered this, an angel of the Lord appeared to him in a dream and said, "Joseph son of David, do not be afraid to take Mary home as your wife, because what is conceived in her is from the Holy Spirit."

10. What does the Bible mean by sexual immorality?

Eph 5:3-5 "But fornication, and all uncleanness, or covetousness, let it not be -- among you, -- neither filthiness, nor foolish talking, nor (course) jesting --: but rather giving of thanks. For this ye know, that no whoremonger, nor unclean person, nor covetous man, who is an idolater, hath any inheritance in the kingdom of Christ and of God." KJV

Lev 20:13-21 "If a man lies with a man as one lies with a woman, both of them have done what is detestable.--- 17 "If a man marries his sister, the daughter of either his father or his mother, and they have sexual relations, it is a disgrace. --- He has dishonoured his sister. "If a man lies with a woman during her monthly period and has sexual relations with her, he has exposed the source of her flow, and she has also uncovered it. Both of them must be cut off from their people. "Do not have sexual relations with the sister of either your mother or your father, for that would dishonour a close relative; both of you would be held responsible. "If a man sleeps with his aunt, he has dishonoured his uncle. They will be held responsible; 21 "If a man marries his brother's wife, it is an act of impurity; he has dishonoured his brother. (NB sex with animals is also forbidden in this passage.)

See also Rom 1:26-28

11. Is Prostitution acceptable?

Prov 6:23-29 "These commands are a lamp, this teaching is a light, --- keeping you from the immoral woman, from the smooth tongue of the wayward wife. Do not lust in your heart after her beauty or let her captivate you with her eyes, for the prostitute reduces you to a loaf of bread, and the adulteress preys upon your very life. Can a man scoop fire into his lap without his clothes being burned? Can a man walk on hot coals without his feet being scorched? So is he who sleeps with another man's wife; no-one who touches her will go unpunished"

1 Cor 6:15-16 "Do you not know that your bodies are members of Christ himself? Shall I then take the members of Christ and unite them with a prostitute? Never! Do you not know that he who unites himself with a prostitute is one with her in body? For it is said, "The two will become one flesh.""

Deut 23:17"There shall be no whore of the daughters of Israel, nor a sodomite of the sons of Israel." KJV

Heb 13:4 "Marriage is honourable in all, and the bed undefiled: but whoremongers and adulterers God will judge." KJV

12. **Should I return to my first husband or wife?** Deut 24:1-4 "If a man -- writes her a certificate of divorce, --- her and sends her from his house, and if after she leaves his house she becomes the wife of another man, and her second husband dislikes her and writes her a certificate of divorce, -- and sends her from his house, or if he dies, then her first husband, who divorced her, is not allowed to marry her again after she has been defiled. That would be detestable in the eyes of the LORD.

13. **Does the Bible condemn without hope all who sin?** No, it always offers forgiveness and reconciliation if we are willing to confess our sin and amend our ways.

1 John 1:8-10 "If we say that we have no sin, we deceive ourselves, and the truth is not in us. If we confess our sins,

he is faithful and just to forgive us our sins, and to cleanse us from all unrighteousness. If we say that we have not sinned, we make him a liar, and his word is not in us." KJV.

14. Who may enjoy sex? Those committed in a marriage relationship.

Prov 5:15-20 "Drink water from your own cistern, running water from your own well. Should your springs overflow in the streets, your streams of water in the public squares? Let them be yours alone, never to be shared with strangers. May your fountain be blessed, and may you rejoice in the wife of your youth. A loving doe, a graceful deer—may her breasts satisfy you always, may you ever be captivated by her love. -- Why be captivated, my son, by an adulteress? Why embrace the bosom of another man's wife?

15. Does the Bible really tell us to enjoy sex? Yes it tells us that sex between married couples is good and enjoyable.

1 Cor 7:3-5 "The husband should fulfil his marital duty to his wife, and likewise the wife to her husband. The wife's body does not belong to her alone but also to her husband. In the same way, the husband's body does not belong to him alone but also to his wife. Do not deprive each other except by mutual consent and for a time, so that you may devote yourselves to prayer. Then come together again so that Satan will not tempt you because of your lack of self-control."

In Poetry the Bible speaks much of love between a husband and wife.

Song 4:4-16 "Thy neck is like the tower of David built for an armoury, whereon there hang a thousand bucklers, all shields of mighty men. Thy two breasts are like two young roes that are twins, which feed among the lilies. Until the day break and the shadows flee away, I will get me to the mountain of myrrh, and to the hill of frankincense. Thou art all fair, my love; there is no spot in thee. Thou hast ravished my heart, my sister, my spouse; thou hast ravished my heart with one of thine eyes, with one chain of thy neck. How fair is thy love, my sister, my spouse! How much better is thy love than wine! And the smell of thine ointments than all spices! Thy lips, O my spouse, drop as the honeycomb: honey and milk are under thy tongue; and the smell of thy garments is like the smell of Lebanon. A garden inclosed is my sister, my spouse; a spring shut up, a fountain sealed. Thy plants are an orchard of pomegranates, with pleasant fruits; camphire, with spikenard, Spikenard and saffron; calamus and cinnamon, with all trees of frankincense; myrrh and aloes, with all the chief spices: A fountain of gardens, a well of living waters, and streams from Lebanon. Awake, O north wind; and come, thou south; blow upon my garden, that the spices thereof may flow out. Let my beloved come into his garden, and eat his pleasant fruits. KJV

Song 5:3-6 "I have taken off my robe—must I put it on again? I have washed my feet—must I soil them again? My lover thrust his hand through the latch-opening; my heart began to pound for him. I arose to open for my lover, and my hands dripped with myrrh, my fingers with flowing myrrh, on the handles of the lock. I opened for my lover.

Song 7:6-10 "How fair and how pleasant art thou, O love, for delights! Thy stature is like to a palm tree, and thy breasts to clusters of grapes. I said, I will go up to the palm tree, I will take hold of the boughs thereof: now also thy breasts shall be as clusters of the vine, and the smell of thy (breath) like apples; And the roof of thy mouth like the best wine --- that goeth down sweetly. -- I am my beloveds, and his desire is toward me. KJV

Song 8:3-4 "His left hand should be under my head, and his right hand should embrace me. I charge you, O daughters of Jerusalem, that ye stir not up, nor awake my love, until he pleases." KJV

16. How do we renew a faltering marriage? We do it by remembering what we have lost, repenting of our faults and returning to the things we did at first. We learn again to put our partner first.

Rev 2:4-5 "I have somewhat against thee, because thou hast left thy first love. Remember therefore from whence thou art fallen, and repent, and do the first works; or else I will come unto thee quickly, -- unless you repent. KJV

1 Cor 7:33"A married man is concerned about -- how he can please his wife"

Eph 5:33 "Each one of you also must love his wife as he loves himself, and the wife must respect her husband."

1 Cor 7:3-5 "The husband should fulfil his marital duty to his wife, and likewise the wife to her husband. The wife's body does not belong to her alone but also to her husband. In the same way, the husband's body does not belong to him alone but also to his wife. Do not deprive each other except by mutual consent and for a time."

17. What does the Bible say about Children? *Ps 127:3-5 "Children are a gift from God; they are his reward. Happy is the man who has his quiver full of them.* **TLB**

To Children, *Deut 5:16 "Honour thy father and thy mother, as the LORD thy God hath commanded thee; that thy days may be prolonged, and that it may go well with thee." KJV*

Eph 6:1-4 "Children, obey your parents in the Lord, for this is right. "Honour your father and mother"-- which is the first commandment with a promise-- "that it may go well with you and that you may enjoy long life on the earth." Fathers, do not exasperate your children; instead, bring them up in the training and instruction of the Lord.

18. How should husband and wife treat each other?
With kindness & respect!
Eph 4:32 "be ye kind one to another, tender hearted, forgiving one another, even as God for Christ's sake hath forgiven you. KJV

Eph 5:28 +33. "Husbands ought to love their wives as their own bodies; he who loves his wife loves himself. Each one of you also must love his wife as he loves himself, and the wife must respect her husband."

Col 3:13-14 "Bear with each other and forgive whatever grievances you may have against one another. Forgive as the Lord forgave you. And over all these virtues put on love, which binds them all together in perfect unity."

19 Is Marriage for life? Yes it is a binding covenant.

Matt 19:5-6 "For this reason a man will leave his father and mother and be united to his wife, and the two will become one flesh'? So they are no longer two, but one. Therefore what God has joined together, let man not separate."

20. Is Polygamy acceptable? No Jesus said, Matt 19:5 *"The* **two** *will* **become one** *flesh'* Paul tells us, *1 Tim 3:2 2 "An overseer, then, must be above reproach, the husband of one wife."* NIV. .

21. Who are these teachings for? They are for everybody but especially those who believe. However I have written mainly with believers in mind.

John 13:17 "Now that you know these things, you will be blessed if you do them."

If you have found these thoughts from the Bible difficult, I remind you that I am not seeking to judge anyone for their life style. As a Minister I write firstly for those who call themselves Christians. As Paul said, *"What business is it of mine to judge those outside the church? 1 Cor 5:12*-13. If we claim to follow Jesus Christ we must live as His word commands. However I am convinced our lives will be better if we live by the standards of God's Word, even if we are not Christians.

A Prayer.

Father, You alone are God, we do not dispute your wisdom but thank you that you have sent your word to guide us in this life and to lead us to eternal life.

We know we can not find your blessing if we disobey your word. Help us now to commit ourselves to living according to your word.

Where we have fallen short of your wisdom forgive us, and as we follow your plan please guide us and place your blessing upon our lives; that we may be the people you intend us to be, we ask this in the name of Christ our Saviour. AMEN.

Stories of Hope.

David and Tina's story. The meeting was over and people were sharing pleasantries as they made their way home. Waiting at the side were a young couple. She was leading her husband who spoke little. The message had touched them deeply and stirred old pains and emotions hidden beneath the surface. She was vivacious, attractive and outgoing; he was slim, quiet and retiring, perhaps less keen to share their story.

Her story began. "We were brought up in a community where faith and faithfulness were very important. People were expected to conform, we married young and for a long while things went well. I don't know if it was because we delayed having children or whether it was work that caused us to drift apart? I only know that I was attracted to a friend at work. We flirted and sent notes to each other. I began to imagine what it would be like to start a new life with him. My heart raced whenever he came near. But the problem was, I did not know if he felt the same way. In the office it seemed that he chose me for special jobs and always seemed to appear in the photo copier room, or take his break at the same time as me. He would brush past my chair and the hairs on my neck would stand on end. There was a passion here that we had lost at home. I know the gossips at the office were beginning to talk, many of them went to my Church but what did that matter to me, we hadn't done anything."

"At home things weren't bad, just boring. It wasn't that we were fighting, just that we did not communicate. Sex was no great event, it was OK but not earth moving and we certainly never gave the time to romancing each other. At night we were tired, and I felt sex was just for sex sake, not an expression of love. He seemed happy enough but I gradually became less responsive."

"At work I felt some small pang of guilt but made my excuses: this was fun, it was daring, intoxicating. Somehow we had become friends without even trying. The problems started when we had an innocent lunch together. I came back and the girls shunned me. My husband was a friend of the boss and the boss was an elder at our Church; he would not want to see David betrayed. My face may have been red but I was not going to be dictated to by those religious hypocrites and prudes. I knew their secrets, how could they judge me. I felt sure God would want me to be happy, perhaps we had married too young, we didn't know our own minds, and how can you decide for a life time at 18 and 19?"

"Then one evening, I was asked to work late. We went for a drink afterwards and then back to the office, to collect some papers. I'm not sure how but as we walked up to his office we were holding hands. He closed the door and we kissed. It was only minutes before clothing came off, and with the radio on in the background, we began to give in to our urge for sex. I had almost no clothes on and his trousers were down when the MD walked into the room. Suddenly this was not fun, it was blind terror. My job, my husband, my family, and my Church were all betrayed in one stupid moment of selfish passion. I was caught in the act of adultery."

"The next day I was called into the board room; my husband was there looking stunned, the Boss, the head of our department, several other board members, and the Pastor of our Church were all there. The only person not present was the man I had been caught with. I learned later he had been transferred to another branch in the next town, a 20 mile drive and he soon got promotion. There was nowhere to hide, I was guilty and shaking to the pit of my stomach. The anger and revulsion that flowed from this group was intense. I felt like a criminal before a western lynch mob. There was no point in defending myself I had no defence. I was caught."

"I don't remember much of what was said, till they turned to the Pastor. He had been at the Church for 20 years. I think there were tears in his eyes; he had married David and I, and evidently felt deeply wounded. Slowly he caught the eye of each person present, all members at one Church or another. "We take the Bible seriously here", he said, "so there is only one thing to do. If you have never sinned then you can be the one who decides Tina's fate." Then he stood and walked slowly to each of the people present starting with the oldest, he only said a few words, but as he did their faces changed. I still don't know what he said perhaps something from the Bible, perhaps something from their past? But they either sat down or left the room. At the end he said: "they don't seem to know what to do, I won't add to your pain but you must determine never to fall into this sin again." I didn't argue I just slumped to the floor.

"We walked to the Pastor's house, David and I. The pain in my husband's voice and continual moving of his arms and legs as if constantly aching was the worst. Today we live in another town. I lost my job, but David and I decided to try again. We went for counselling and began to build a stronger marriage. We are only in out thirties now and I tell you this, I will never betray my husband again, who stood by me when I did not deserve it, and I will always thank God for a second chance at life. I have learned that Christians aren't always holy people; they are people with a past which has been forgiven. Like the woman in the Bible story I found Jesus did not condemn me."

The hall was now empty; we had spoken for an hour. I turned to her husband as asked: "how is your marriage now?" Two emotions seemed to flow inside him, one showed a wound which was still painful to remember, the other an overwhelming love for his wife. He made his excuses and they left after prayer. They had to relieve grandma from caring for their 5 year old daughter, and I understood that they had

found a new hope and a future together. I don't see them often as I no longer live close to their town.
See John 8:1-12.

Joanne's story. I knew Joanne some 15 years ago. She was a woman in her mid forties though the freshness of youth had left her face and features; she looked after herself, and was still attractive with auburn hair and a wonderful enticing smile. She was friendly and outgoing, but made friends with men more easily than women. I found her one day shopping in the local market, she was having trouble with too many carrier bags so we walked together and I carried some of the load.

"Have you met Jim yet" she said? "No" I replied, "is Jim your son?" She smiled at me with a feigned patience; I was a minister and could not understand the intricacies of her relationships. Jim was her new boyfriend, Geoff her partner had recently left her. "What happened," I enquired. "Something about taking back soiled goods" she laughed but the laughter only hid the pain.

We rested at the bus stop, no busses as usual and she shared her story. "When I was a young girl I turned every boy's head. Got a bit of a reputation at school, all the boys wanted to take me for a walk in the park, or get the last dance at the party. It was fun but I was looking for that special one. I was only 16 when I had my first real relationship; it lasted about 20 minutes in the back of a Ford."

Then she turned to me with a real intensity and asked: "is that really all men want, just a quick thrill and a naked woman?" "Some men", I replied. "I don't seem to have much luck with men," she said. "My first husband drank; he left for a teenager just out of school. My second died in the Falklands; John was a good man perhaps we would have made it? It was OK being a widow for a while people had sympathy, but now I go to the market late because after 5 husbands the women just talk; they think I'm immoral, they haven't lived my life." "God knows about the pain" I gently replied. She almost got up and left, "what does God know of me" she said? We stood and walked on. The day was grey and cold, and her house was only half a mile from ours. Joanne had even been to Church a few times but never seemed to settle.

She continued, "When I met Harry I thought it was going to be fine. We married quickly but he hated the fact I had been married before and when we had no children he soon left, two years of separation and no contesting the divorce when the decree Nissi came through. I did get the house, but a house with no man is empty. In my thirties I did try to review my life, went to a few night classes and got a better job. One of the younger men dated me for a while, he was only after one thing and when I mentioned marriage he stopped calling. After that let down I got a proposal from an older man. When you are desperate you will do anything. He was 58 and I was 36, how could that work out? Six months we were married."

"Four marriages" I sighed. "No, five", she said. "I met Ed through an internet chat room. We did a Britney Spears, married in Las Vegas on Saturday, blew my savings to go out and meet him, divorced on Wednesday, he was really scary. Geoff who came to Church with me wasn't really my husband nor is Jim, but you never know? Most people don't give me the time of day and don't believe my 'tall tales'."

We had arrived at her house; I placed the shopping on the step. Jim was digging in the back garden and Joanne introduced me as the Vicar, I never like that. Most men avoid outward shows of religion; the job of a minister is something they can't quite understand. Jim worked on and we sat at the kitchen table. Joanne's real trouble was she felt of little value. No man had ever valued her above her body and now as she aged she felt worthless. The idea that someone could love her for herself was miles from her mind.

I hate sounding religious but I said, "Perhaps it's time for you to ask God's help." Her face froze, to tell the truth I still don't know what she was thinking? She may have wanted to ask me to leave, or even thought that I was joking? She could have been thinking: "does God really want the likes of me?" I asked her if I could show her a Bible story and there at the kitchen table, we read together the story of the woman at the well. (John 4:5-42) We saw how Jesus knew all she had done and still offered her a new and refreshing life. "Pity Jesus isn't here now", she said. We shared a brief prayer and next Sunday she and Jim were in Church. I think it took three weeks before the penny dropped and they understood that Christ really cared for them and was waiting at the door of their lives to be invited in. They went home and one Sunday night after service knelt by their bed and asked Christ to forgive their past and come into their lives. Yes, they married not at my Church but they chose the registry office, and both of them found that they were so much more valuable than just for their looks. Jesus said, *"Behold, I stand at the door, and knock: if any man hears my voice, and opens the door, I will come in to him, and will sup with him, and he with me." Rev 3:20. KJV modernised.*

Julie's story. "I ran away from home at 17, no one seemed to care. Dad left us when I was just a child, and life out there had to be so much better. No one plans to become a prostitute, but when you have no qualifications and a real need, it happens. The men are nobodies; usually married, just a meal ticket. I tried to keep off drugs but my room mate was hooked and it was too easy. I've seen people die and seen ugly painful diseases for lads as well as girls. After six months I hated life and I hated myself. I even harmed myself sometimes."

"What changed me? It was Steve, a youth worker from the Church. They opened a youth coffee bar. I just went a few times and then promised to come to the Church, what could it hurt? I went once and they invited me to do Alpha. They said it explained what Christianity was really all about and gave a free meal. I nearly didn't come back, my work and this Church didn't seem to fit together; and then they held a special meeting on the Friday night, a "Holy Spirit" night. I can't explain it but God was in the place, I knew he was there and I knew he loved me. The sense was overwhelming, I found myself along with others kneeling at the communion table with the tears flooding down my cheeks. I felt ashamed but accepted at the same time. The minister read out this verse from the Bible *"Her sins, which are many, are forgiven; for she loved much: but to whom little is forgiven, the same loves little."* Then he said, *"Your sins are forgiven. Your faith hath saved you; go in peace." Luke 7:47-50 KJV.*

These verses were written for a woman who met Jesus so many years ago but when I heard them that night they were for me. The Church helped me get into a rehab programme and when I finish I want to go back and help Steve at the café. I'm even planning to take night classes and my Mum has been down to visit me. I have a family again. Read Luke 7:36-50.

Ben's Story. I had known Ben since our early days at School, as a teenager his two passions were girls and sport, but now Ben was 21, he sat on the edge of the bed, literally sobbing from the depths of his soul. For three years he and Millie had been inseparable, but today he had made the hardest decision of his life. He had just finished with girl he expected to marry and there was no chance of reconciliation. The clash was inevitable but shattering.

He and Millie had known each other at school but they really became close when they began to work together. The problem was simple, they fell in love at 17 and slowly but increasingly became physically involved. They were inexperienced, but genuinely passionate about each other. Then after about six months together Ben came to faith in Christ, the change was instant. His attendance at Sunday school probably prepared the way, but in one night of conversation with a close Christian friend, he knelt and gave his life to Christ. Ben was still passionate about Millie but the consuming desire of his life was to know more of Christ.

The difficulty was how to turn back the clock? Sunday by Sunday he attended the little Gospel Hall, yet each time he and Millie were alone his instincts pulled in a different direction. The idea of self control had never been part of his thinking before; he was used to pushing each situation as far as it would go. They had gone further than simple petting and it was only circumstances and over excitement that had kept them from going all the way. Now 18 months later Ben was at Bible School, but the habits of three years together were hard to break. Each time the met, passions were enflamed and they went further than modesty dictated. The next day a sense of guilt and shame followed. Ben genuinely prayed for forgiveness but he was finding it impossible to serve his passions and God at the same time. The choice had to be made, give in to passion or give in to God. If passion won, Ben's faith would always take second place. The truth is Ben's track record of faithfulness was not good and if he lost his faith there was little chance that he would be a faithful husband to Millie. He was always searching for something better, and now for the first time he had some realistic answers in his Christian faith.

It was really a battle of character versus temptation and the coin was in the air. Finally the decision had to be made; the relationship which had started so innocently had been polluted by premature intimacy. Perhaps if Millie had shared this desire to follow God, things would have been different, but she found all this excitement about faith in Christ confusing and her parents opposed her attendance at Church.

As the first year at Bible school drew to a close, they split and went their separate ways. The ring was returned to the jewellers and all their hopes were dashed.

(Teenagers often argue that it is fine to sleep together as long as you are committed to each other. Ben and Millie were committed for three years, but temptation actually spoiled their relationship, it did not enrich it. If they had gone "all the way," and then separated they would have carried that experience into their marriage and would run the risk of comparing their married partner with the lover of their youth, which is dangerous and destructive. We all need to be able to trust our partners sexually. I remember well the man who came to me seeking a Ministers advice, his wife was heavily pregnant and he confessed that he was not sure that he still loved her. He asked if he should return to his former long term lover, leaving his wife and soon to be born child? If we can not answer that question we have no moral integrity at all.) Statistics show us that the average length of time a couple stay together as live in lovers is only 19 months. When the break up comes they carry the pain of the past into the new relationship. The "Sex and the City" generation is reaping a bitter harvest from broken relationships. Far better to start clean and new with your husband or wife and not bring old baggage, old memories and old hurts into your relationship.

Millie married a local boy and they made a life together outside of the Christian faith. When Ben returned to Bible School the next year, he also found a new start; as he began his second year, a young woman who shared a passion for God began her first year. Today Ben is a Pastor and his wife stands with him in the ministry. The decision he made to go God's way, became one of the decisive turning points in his life. It prepared the way for a new start in a fresh relationship based on the right priorities. See Matthew 6:24, James 1:12-16.

The idea that God doesn't care for those who get it wrong is never found in the Bible, Jesus came to seek and to save those who are lost. He did not call the good people but the ones who had got it wrong. The first two stories are slightly dramatised but are based on people I have personally known, the third is from a testimony I heard, the last shared with Ben's permission. God mends broken lives, and accepts us back, the price is that we must confess the sin in our past, turn away from what we have done wrong, and as the early disciples did "Come and follow Jesus."

The permissive society says seek self-fulfilment, the only rule is enjoyment. Do what you want they say; "Sex is a gift to be celebrated between consenting adults." This has caused heartache for so many people. God says chastity before marriage and faithfulness within marriage is the only true way to personal happiness and a stable family life. It is also the best protection against sexually transmitted diseases!

Sin can never lead to happiness; it promises to please but it lies, it only brings misery and emptiness. God's way brings healing of relationships, of mind and of Soul. Jesus alone offers peace of mind. *He said, "Peace I leave with you, my peace I give unto you: not as the world gives, I give unto you. Let not your heart be troubled, neither let it be afraid." John 14:27 KJV*

We can not build a strong marriage on the wrong foundation. Right thinking is the start of a right relationship. Our love must be a matter of deep devotion and firm commitment. I trust this book will help you think and act in love. Remember talk is cheap, what you need is love in action. Be fully prepared to forgive the hurts of the past and learn to communicate without blaming each other. We know we have fully forgiven when we no longer mention what the other person did to hurt us! If God is willing to forgive and never mention out faults, this must be out attitude to the one we love. See your own faults as well as theirs and remember you have made a vow, "For better for worse, for richer for poorer, in sickness and in health, till death do us part."

Do use the questions in this book as an aid to conversation, speak together with great patience and always be ready to listen and respond to the needs of your loved one. Then I feel sure you will **build a better marriage;** one which stands the test of time.   Don't give up, this is the most important relationship you have on this earth, work at it, the rewards are life long.

I pray that God will use this little book to strengthen many marriages. If you are ready now to ask God's help, go back to the prayer on pages 54 and 55 and talk to God. God has covenanted to accept us as we came to him through faith in His Son Jesus. Marriage is a covenant and we may seek His guidance and wisdom in our marriages. If we have never decided to follow God's way, now is the time to commit our future to his care and to follow Him. If you are serious about going God's way and you have no Church of your own, you will need to find one where you can learn of our Lord and Saviour Jesus Christ, Christians are never solitary believers but are called to be part of the bride of Christ, the community of people who bear His name, CHRISTIANS.

The Lord Bless you in your marriage and in your future,
Rev D Kevin Jones, Methodist Minister.

A Prayer.
Dear Lord you are our guide and friend, today you are writing the story of our lives, keep us from a foolish stubborn heart which wanders away from you, where we have gone our own ways please forgive and restores us to a life lived for your purposes.

As you mended the lives of these people so reach out into our lives and mend what is broken, heal us in body soul and spirit that our lives, and our marriages may know the fullness of joy you intend. We acknowledge our hope is in Jesus and today we ask his help.

Thank you father for loving us, receive the praise that come through our lives lived to your glory, **AMEN**.

Also available:-

The Seven last word's of Christ. A complete lent study course, focusing on the significance of the last word's spoken by Christ from the cross.
- Available for individual or groups study.
- Includes a 50 day reading plan and commentary, for lent and Easter week. "Through the life of Jesus in Chronological order."
- Suggested Sermon Outline, for lent & Easter.
- Questions and prayers for use in group study.
- Choice of hymns & songs for each week.

Available in CD Rom or Disk Format for PC from "Heart of Oak;" also on line at www.jerseypassion.org then look at additional resources to down load the PDF file (464 kb), under the title **"The purpose of the Passion."**

Also Available: **"The Bridge to Eternity"** From **Amazon** ISBN 0-9549462-2-7 £7-50 or direct form Heart of Oak.

An in depth exploration of the book of Hebrews; concentrating on the supremacy of Christ, and the significance of his sacrifice for today. First published as a series in the "Headway" Magazine 2004.

Available from "Heart of Oak" publishers, 22 Chapel lane, Banks, Southport, Lancashire, PR9 8EY

www.ingramcontent.com/pod-product-compliance
Lightning Source LLC
Chambersburg PA
CBHW032147040426
42449CB00005B/430